Dogs 101: A Guide to American Kennel Club Breed Groups, Vol. 3 - The Working Group

Jacob Cleveland

Six Degrees Books. This book was created and put into distribution by a team of dedicated editors and subject matter experts using open source and proprietary publishing tools. The name "Six Degrees Books" is indicative of our desire to make it easy for people to find valuable, but not readily apparent, relationships between pieces of digital content and compile that information into helpful and interesting books.

Curation is King. One of the advantages to the way we publish books is that our content is up to date and written by dedicated subject matter experts from all over the world. By adding a layer of careful screening and curatorial attention to this, we are able to offer a book that is relevant, informative and unique.

We are looking to expand our team: If you are interested to be a Six Degrees editor and get paid for your subject matter expertise - please visit www.sixdegreesbooks.com.

Contents

Articles

References

Breed Groups (dog)

A **Breed Group** is a categorization of related breeds of animal by an overseeing organization, used to organize the showing of animals. In dogs, kennel clubs define the *Breed Groups* and decide which dog breeds are to be included in each *Breed Group*. The Fédération Cynologique Internationale *Breed Groups* are used to organize dogs for international competition. *Breed Groups* often have the names of, and are loosely based on, ancestral dog types of modern dog breeds.

Recognized Breed Groups

International

The Fédération Cynologique Internationale makes sure that dogs in its 84 member countries can compete together, by establishing common nomenclature and making sure that pedigrees are mutually recognized in all the member countries. So internationally, dog breeds are organized in ten groups, each with subsections according to breed type and origin.

- **Group 1 - Sheepdogs and Cattle Dogs (except Swiss Cattle Dogs)**
- **Group 2 Pinscher and Schnauzer - Molossoid Breeds - Swiss Mountain and Cattle Dogs**
  - Section 1: Pinscher and Schnauzer type
  - Section 2: Molossoid breeds
  - Section 3: Swiss Mountain and Cattle Dogs
- **Group 3 Terriers**
  - Section 1: Large and medium-sized Terriers
  - Section 2: Small-sized Terriers
  - Section 3: Bull type Terriers
  - Section 4: Toy Terriers
- **Group 4 Dachshunds**
- **Group 5 Spitz and Primitive types**
  - Section 1: Nordic Sledge Dogs
  - Section 2: Nordic Hunting Dogs
  - Section 3: Nordic Watchdogs and Herders
  - Section 4: European Spitz
  - Section 5: Asian Spitz and related breeds
  - Section 6: Primitive type
  - Section 7: Primitive type - Hunting Dogs
  - Section 8: Primitive type Hunting Dogs with a ridge on the back

- **Group 6 Scenthounds and Related Breeds**
  - Section 1: Scenthounds
  - Section 2: Leash (scent) Hounds
  - Section 3: Related breeds (Dalmatian and Rhodesian Ridgeback)
- **Group 7 Pointing Dogs**
  - Section 1: Continental Pointing Dogs
  - Section 2: British and Irish Pointers and Setters
- **Group 8 Retrievers - Flushing Dogs - Water Dogs**
  - Section 1: Retrievers
  - Section 2: Flushing Dogs
  - Section 3: Water Dogs
- **Group 9 Companion and Toy Dogs**
  - Section 1: Bichons and related breeds
  - Section 2: Poodle
  - Section 3: Small Belgian Dogs
  - Section 4: Hairless Dogs
  - Section 5: Tibetan breeds
  - Section 6: Chihuahueñ o
  - Section 7: English Toy Spaniels
  - Section 8: Japan Chin and Pekingese
  - Section 9: Continental Toy Spaniel
  - Section 10: Kromfohrländer
  - Section 11: Small Molossian type Dogs
- **Group 10 Sighthounds**
  - Section 1: Long-haired or fringed Sighthounds
  - Section 2: Rough-haired Sighthounds
  - Section 3: Short-haired Sighthounds

The Kennel Club

The Kennel Club (UK) is the original and oldest kennel club; it is not a member of the Fédération Cynologique Internationale. For The Kennel Club, dogs are placed in the following groups:

- Hound Group
- Gundog Group
- Terrier Group
- Utility Group
- Working Group

- Pastoral Group
- Toy Group

Working is here meant to indicate dogs that are not hunting dogs that work directly for people, such as police dogs, search and rescue dogs, and others. It does not imply that other types of dogs do not work. Dogs that work with livestock are in the Pastoral Group.

Australia and New Zealand

The Australian National Kennel Council and the New Zealand Kennel Club recognize similar groups to The Kennel Club.

Australian National Kennel Council recognized Breed Groups:

- Group 1 (Toys)
- Group 2 (Terriers)
- Group 3 (Gundogs)
- Group 4 (Hounds)
- Group 5 (Working Dogs)
- Group 6 (Utility)
- Group 7 (Non Sporting)

New Zealand Kennel Club recognized Breed Groups:

- Toy Group
- Terrier Group
- Gundogs
- Hound Group
- Working Group
- Utility Group
- Non Sporting Group

North America

The Canadian Kennel Club and the two major kennel clubs in the United States have similar groups, although they may not include the same dogs in the same groupings. Canadian Kennel Club recognized Breed Groups:

- Group 1, Sporting Dogs
- Group 2, Hounds
- Group 3, Working Dogs
- Group 4, Terriers
- Group 5, Toys
- Group 6, Non-Sporting
- Group 7, Herding

American Kennel Club recognized Breed Groups:

- Sporting Group
- Hound Group
- Working Group
- Terrier Group
- Toy Group
- Non-Sporting Group
- Herding Group

United Kennel Club (US) recognized Breed Groups:

- Companion Dog Group
- Guardian Dog Group
- Gun Dog Group
- Herding Dog Group
- Northern Breed Group
- Scenthound Group
- Sighthound & Pariah Group
- Terrier Group

Other

The major national kennel club for each country will organize breeds in breed groups. The naming and organization of *Breed Groups* may vary from country to country. In addition, some rare new breeds or newly documented traditional breeds may be awaiting approval by a given kennel club, and may not yet be assigned to a particular *Breed Group*.

In addition to the major registries, there are a nearly infinite number of sporting clubs, breed clubs, minor kennel clubs, and internet-based breed registries and dog registration businesses in which breeds may be organized into whatever Breed Group the club, minor registry, or dog business may devise.

See also

- Dog type
- Dog breed
- Conformation show
- General Specials

External links

- http://www.dogsonline.com
- http://www.dogsindepth.com/index.html Dog Breed Groups from dogsindepth.com the online dog encyclopedia
- http://www.u-c-i.de/

American Kennel Club

The **American Kennel Club** (or **AKC**) is a registry of purebred dog pedigrees in the United States. Beyond maintaining its pedigree registry, this kennel club also promotes and sanctions events for purebred dogs, including the Westminster Kennel Club Dog Show, an annual event which predates the official forming of the AKC, the National Dog Show, and the AKC/Eukanuba National Championship. Unlike most other country's kennels clubs, the AKC is not part of the Fédération Cynologique Internationale (World Canine Organization).

Dog registration

The AKC is not the only registry of purebred dogs, but it is the only non-profit registry and the one with which most Americans are familiar. Founded in 1884, the AKC is the largest purebred dog registry in the world. Along with its nearly 5,000 licensed and member clubs and affiliated organizations, the AKC advocates for the purebred dog as a family companion, advances canine health and well-being, works to protect the rights of all dog owners and promotes responsible dog ownership. An example of dogs registered elsewhere in the U.S. is the National Greyhound Association which registers racing greyhounds (which are legally not considered "pets").

For a purebred dog to be registered with the AKC, the dog's parents must be registered with the AKC as the same breed, and the litter in which the dog is born must be registered with the AKC. If the dog's parents are not registered with the AKC or the litter is not registered, special registry research by the AKC is necessary for the AKC to determine if the dog is eligible for AKC registration. Once a determination of eligibility is met, either by litter application or registry research, the dog can be registered as purebred by the AKC.To register a mixed breed dog with AKC as a Canine Partner, you may go to the AKC website and enroll the dog via an online form. Once registered, your mixed breed dog will be eligible to compete in the AKC Agility, Obedience and AKC Rally® Events. 2010 Most Popular Dogs in the U.S.

1. Labrador Retriever

2. German Shepherd Dog

3. Yorkshire Terrier

4. Golden Retriever

5. Beagle

6. Boxer

7. Bulldog

8. Dachshund

9. Poodle

10. Shih Tzu

Registration indicates only that the dog's parents were registered as one recognized breed; it does not necessarily indicate that the dog comes from healthy or show-quality blood lines. Nor is registration necessarily a reflection on the quality of the breeder or how the puppy was raised. Registration is necessary only for breeders (so they can sell registered puppies) or for purebred conformation show or purebred dog sports participation. Registration can be obtained by mail or online at their website.

AKC and health

Even though the AKC supports some canine health research and has run advertising campaigns implying that the AKC is committed to healthy dogs, the AKC's role in furthering dog health is controversial. Temple Grandin maintains that the AKC's standards only regulate physical appearance, not emotional or behavioral health. The AKC has no health standards for breeding. The only breeding restriction is age (a dog can be no younger than 8 months.) Furthermore, the AKC prohibits clubs from imposing stricter regulations, that is, an AKC breed club cannot require a higher breeding age, hip dysplasia ratings, genetic tests for inheritable diseases, or any other restrictions. Parent clubs do have the power to define the looks of the breed, or breed standard. Parent club may also restrict participation in non-regular events or classes such as Futurities or Maturities to only those dogs meeting their defined criteria. This enables those non-regular events to require health testing, DNA sampling, instinct/ability testing and other outlined requirements as established by the hosting club of the non-regular event.

As a result, attention to health among breeders is purely voluntary. By contrast, many dog clubs outside the US do require health tests of breeding dogs. The German Shepherd Club of Germany [1], for example, requires hip and elbow X-rays in addition to other tests before a dog can be bred. Such breeding restrictions are not allowed in AKC member clubs. As a result, some US breeders have established parallel registries or health databases outside of the AKC; for example, the Berner Garde [2] established such a database in 1995 after genetic diseases reduced the average lifespan of a Bernese Mountain Dog to 7 years. The Swiss Bernese Mountain Dog club introduced mandatory hip X-rays in 1971.

For these, and other reasons, a small number of breed clubs have not yet joined the AKC so they can maintain stringent health standards, but, in general, the breeders' desire to show their dogs at AKC shows such as the Westminster Dog Show has won out over these concerns.

Contrary to most western nations organized under the International Kennel Federation (of which the AKC is not a member), the AKC has not removed docked tails and cropped ears from the requirements of many AKC breed standards, even though this practice is opposed in the U.S. by the American Veterinary Medical Association, and banned by law in many other countries.

The Club has also been criticized for courting large scale commercial breeders.

Purebred Alternative Listing Program / Indefinite Listing Privilege Program

The Purebred Alternative Listing Program (PAL), formerly the Indefinite Listing Privilege Program (ILP), is an AKC program that provides purebred dogs who may not have been eligible for registration a chance to register "alternatively" (formerly "indefinitely"). There are various reasons why a purebred dog might not be eligible for registration; for example, the dog may be the product of an unregisterable litter, or have unregisterable parents. Many dogs enrolled in the PAL and ILP programs were adopted from animal shelters or rescue groups, in which case the status of the dog's parents is unknown. Dogs enrolled in PAL/ILP may participate in AKC companion and performance activities, but not conformation. Enrollees of the program receive various benefits, including a subscription to *Family Dog* Magazine, a certificate for their dog's place in the PAL, and information about AKC Pet Healthcare and microchipping. Dogs that were registered under the ILP program keep their original numbers.

AKC National Championship

The AKC/Eukanuba National Championship is an annual event held in both Tampa, FL, and Long Beach, CA. The show is by invitation only. The dogs invited to the show have either finished their championship from the bred-by-exhibitor class or ranked in the Top 25 of their breed. The show can often be seen on major television stations.

Open foundation stock

The Foundation Stock Service (FSS) is an AKC program for breeds not yet accepted by the AKC for full recognition, and not yet in the AKC's Miscellaneous class. The AKC FSS requires that at least the parents of the registered animal are known. The AKC will not grant championship points to dogs in these breeds until the stud book is closed and the breed is granted full recognition.

Activities

The AKC sanctions events in which dogs and handlers can compete. These are divided into three areas:

- Conformation shows
  - Junior Showmanship
- Companion events, in which all registered and PAL/ILP dogs can compete. These include:
  - Obedience trials
  - Tracking trials
  - Dog agility
  - Rally obedience
- Performance events, which are limited to certain entrants; PAL/ILP dogs of the correct breed are usually eligible:
  - Coonhound events (coonhounds; no PAL/ILP dogs)
  - Field trials (hounds)
  - Earthdog trials (small terriers and Dachshunds)
  - Sheepdog trials (herding tests) (herding breeds, Rottweilers, and Samoyeds)
  - Hunt tests (most dogs in the Sporting Groups and Standard Poodles)
  - Lure coursing (sighthounds only)
  - Working Dog Sport (obedience, tracking, protection) German Shepherds, Doberman Pinschers, Rottweilers, Bouvier des Flandres

AKC policy toward working dog sport events that include protection phases, such as Schutzhund, has changed according to prevailing public sentiment in the United States. In 1990, as well-publicized dog attacks were driving public fear against many breeds, the AKC issued a ban on protection sports for all of its member clubs. After the terrorist attacks of 9/11/2001, Americans began to take a more positive attitude toward well-trained protection dogs, and in July 2003 the AKC decided to allow member clubs to hold a limited number of protection events with prior written permission. In 2006 the AKC released rules for its own Working Dog Sport events, very similar to Schutzhund.

In 2007, the American Kennel Club accepted an invitation from the Mexican Kennel Club to participate in the Fédération Cynologique Internationale World Dog Show in Mexico City.

Recognized breeds

As of July 2009, the AKC fully recognizes 163 breeds with 12 additional breeds granted partial status in the Miscellaneous class. Another 62 rare breeds can be registered in its Foundation Stock Service.

The AKC divides dog breeds into seven *groups*, one *class*, and the Foundation Stock Service, consisting of the following (as of July 2009):

- Sporting Group: 28 breeds developed as bird dogs. Includes Pointers, Retrievers, Setters, and Spaniels.
- Hound Group: 25 breeds developed to hunt using sight (sighthounds) or scent (scent hounds). Includes Greyhounds and Beagles.
- Working Group: 26 large breeds developed for a variety of jobs, including guarding property, guarding livestock, or pulling carts. Includes Siberian Huskies and Bernese Mountain Dogs.
- Terrier Group: 27 feisty breeds some of which were developed to hunt vermin and to dig them from their burrows or lairs. Size ranges from the tiny Cairn Terrier to the large Airedale Terrier.
- Toy Group: 21 small companion breeds Includes Toy Poodles and Pekineses.
- Non-Sporting Group: 17 breeds that do not fit into any of the preceding categories, usually larger than Toy dogs. Includes Bichon Frises and Miniature Poodles.
- Herding Group: 22 breeds developed to herd livestock. Includes Rough Collies and Belgian Shepherds.
- Best in Show:over 150 breeds All Breeds
- Miscellaneous Class: 11 breeds that have advanced from FSS but that are not yet fully recognized. After a period of time that ensures that good breeding practices are in effect and that the gene pool for the breed is ample, the breed is moved to one of the seven preceding groups.
- Foundation Stock Service (FSS) Program: 62 breeds. This is a breed registry in which breeders of rare breeds can record the birth and parentage of a breed that they are trying to establish in the United States; these dogs provide the *foundation stock* from which eventually a fully recognized breed might result. These breeds cannot participate in AKC events until at least 150 individual dogs are registered; thereafter, competition in various events is then provisional.

The AKC Board of Directors appointed a committee in October, 2007, to evaluate the current alignment of breeds within the seven variety groups. Reasons for the action included the growing number of breeds in certain groups, and the make-up of breeds within certain groups. The number of groups and group make-up has been modified in the past, providing precedent for this action. The Group Realignment Committee completed their report in July, 2008.

The committee recommended that the seven variety groups be replaced with ten variety groups. If this proposal is approved, the Hound Group would be divided into "Scent Hounds" and "Sight Hounds"; the Sporting Group would be divided into "Sporting Group – Pointers and Setters" and "Sporting Group –

Retrievers and Spaniels"; a new group called the "Northern Group" would be created; and the Non-Sporting Group would be renamed the "Companion Group". The Northern Group would be populated by Northern/Spitz breeds, consisting of the Norwegian Elkhound, Akita, Alaskan Malamute, Siberian Husky, Samoyed, American Eskimo, Chinese Shar-Pei, Chow Chow, Finnish Spitz, Keeshond, Schipperke, Shiba Inu and Swedish Vallhund. In addition, the Italian Greyhound is proposed to be moved to the Sight Hound Group, and the Dalmatian is proposed to be moved to the Working Group.

See also: American Kennel Club Groups

Other AKC programs

The AKC also offers the Canine Good Citizen program. This program tests dogs of any breed (including mixed breed) or type, registered or not, for basic behavior and temperament suitable for appearing in public and living at home.

The AKC also supports Canine Health with the Canine Health Foundation http://www.akcchf.org/

Another AKC affiliate is AKC Companion Animal Recovery (AKC CAR), the nation's largest not-for-profit pet identification and 24/7 recovery service provider. AKC CAR is a leading distributor of pet microchips in the U.S. and a participant in AAHA's free Pet Microchip Lookup tool.

AKC and legislation

The AKC tracks all dog related legislation in the United States, lobbies lawmakers and issues legislative alerts on the internet asking for citizens to contact public officials. They are particularly active in combating breed-specific legislation such as bans on certain breeds considered dangerous. They also combat most legislation to protect animals such as breed-limit restrictions and anti-puppy mill legislation. While they argue that their motive is to protect legitimate breeders and the industry, many argue their incentive is purely financial.

See also

- List of dog breeds
- United Kennel Club
- DOGNY
- American Dog Club
- World Wide Kennel Club
- List of Kennel Clubs by Country

External links

- Official website [3]
- AKC CAR's Official website [4]
- 2007 Registration Data [5]
- The Politics of Dogs: Criticism of Policies of AKC [6] The Atlantic, 1990
- Digging into the AKC: Taking cash for tainted dogs [7] The Philadelphia Inquirer, 1995
- Doogle.Info Worldwide online dog database and pedigree [8]

Working Group (dogs)

Working Group is the name of a breed Group of dogs, used by kennel clubs to classify a defined collection of dog breeds. Most major English-language kennel clubs include a *Working Group*, although different kennel clubs may not include the same breeds in their *Working Group*. *Working Group* does not define one particular type of dog. It is not a scientific classification. *Working Group* is not a term used by the international kennel club association, the Fédération Cynologique Internationale, which more finely divides its breed groupings by dog type and breed history.

Working dogs

There are as many types of work for dogs as there are types of dogs. Lapdogs may *work* as therapy dogs, herding dogs may *work* livestock, and guard dogs may *work* at defense of people or property. Most dogs today are kept as pets rather than for any particular work. Modern purebred breeds developed from large guardian, herding and Spitz type dogs are usually quick to learn, and these intelligent, capable animals make solid companions. Their considerable dimensions and strength alone, however, make many working dogs unsuitable as pets for average families. By virtue of their size alone, these dogs must be properly trained.

Working Group breeds

In general, kennel clubs assign larger breeds that are engaged in some sort of physically active work to their *Working Group*. In areas of the world where livestock production is economically important, pastoral dogs are placed in the *Working Group*. In the rest of the world, such dogs are placed in a Herding Group or Pastoral Group, and dogs that were traditionally bred for guarding, rescue, police or messenger work, as well as large Spitz type dogs, are placed in the *Working Group*. These breeds may also be placed in a kennel club's Utility Group.

Working Group breeds as defined by major kennel clubs

The Kennel Club (UK) Working Group	Canadian Kennel Club Working Dogs Group	American Kennel Club Working Group	Australian National Kennel Council Working Dogs Group	New Zealand Kennel Club Working Group
Alaskan Malamute	Akita	Akita	Australian Cattle Dog	Australian Cattle Dog
Beauceron	Alaskan Malamute	Alaskan Malamute	Australian Kelpie	Australian Kelpie
Bernese Mountain Dog	Bernese Mountain Dog	Anatolian Shepherd Dog	Australian Shepherd	Australian Shepherd
Bouvier Des Flandres	Boxer	Boxer	Bearded Collie	Australian Stumpy Tail Cattle Dog
Boxer	Bullmastiff	Bernese Mountain Dog	Belgian Shepherd (Groenendael)	Bearded Collie
Bullmastiff	Canaan Dog	Black Russian Terrier	Belgian Shepherd (Laekinois)	Belgian Shepherd Dog (Groenendael, Tervuren, Laekenois, Malinois)
Canadian Eskimo Dog	Canadian Eskimo Dog	Boxer	Belgian Shepherd (Malinois)	Bergamasco Shepherd Dog
Dobermann	Cane Corso	Bullmastiff	Belgian Shepherd (Tervueren)	Border Collie
Dogue De Bordeaux	Doberman Pinscher	Doberman Pinscher	Bergamasco Shepherd Dog	Bouvier Des Flandres
Entlebucher Mountain Dog	Entlebucher Mountain Dog	Dogue de Bordeaux	Border Collie	Briard
German Pinscher	Eurasier	German Pinscher	Bouvier Des Flandres	Collie (Rough)
Giant Schnauzer	Great Dane	Giant Schnauzer	Briard	Collie (Smooth)
Great Dane	Great Pyrenees	Great Dane	Collie (Rough)	Finnish Lapphund
Greenland Dog	Greenland Dog	Great Pyrenees	Collie (Smooth)	German Shepherd Dog
Hovawart	Karelian Bear Dog	Greater Swiss Mountain Dog	Finnish Lapphund	Komondor
Leonberger	Komondor	Komondor	German Shepherd Dog	Kuvasz
Mastiff	Kuvasz	Kuvasz	Hungarian Puli	Maremma Sheepdog
Neapolitan Mastiff	Leonberger	Mastiff	Komondor	Norwegian Buhund
Newfoundland	Mastiff	Neapolitan Mastiff	Kuvasz	Old English Sheepdog
Portuguese Water Dog	Newfoundland	Newfoundland	Maremma Sheepdog	Polish Lowland Sheepdog

Pyrenean Mastiff	Portuguese Water Dog	Portuguese Water Dog	Norwegian Buhund	Puli
Rottweiler	Rottweiler	Rottweiler	Old English Sheepdog	Pumi
Russian Black Terrier	Samoyed	Russian Black Terrier	Polish Lowland Sheepdog	Shetland Sheepdog
St. Bernard	Schnauzer (Giant)	Saint Bernard	Pumi	
Siberian Husky	Schnauzer (Standard)	Samoyed	Shetland Sheepdog	Swedish Lapphund
Tibetan Mastiff	Siberian Husky	Siberian Husky	Stumpy Tail Cattle Dog	Swedish Vallhund
	St. Bernard	Standard Schnauzer	Swedish Lapphund	Welsh Corgi (Cardigan)
		Tibetan Mastiff	Swedish Vallhund	Welsh Corgi (Pembroke)
			Welsh Corgi (Cardigan)	
			Welsh Corgi (Pembroke)	
			White Swiss Shepherd Dog	

Photographs

Fédération Cynologique Internationale working groups

The Fédération Cynologique Internationale does not include a group title "Working Group"; its groups "Sheepdogs and Cattle Dogs (except Swiss Cattle Dogs)", "Spitz and Primitive types", and "Pinscher and Schnauzer - Molossoid Breeds - Swiss Mountain and Cattle Dogs and Other Breeds" groups include many of the breeds lumped together in various kennel clubs' *Working Group*s.

See also

- Breed Groups (dog)
- Working dog includes all types of working dogs
- Utility Group

American Akita

The **American Akita**, often called simply **Akita**, is a dog breed from the mountainous northern regions of Japan. The American Akita is considered a separate breed from the Akita Inu (Japanese Akita) in many countries around the world, with the notable exceptions of the United States and Canada. In the US and Canada, both the American Akita and the Akita Inu are considered a single breed with differences in type rather than two separate breeds. Note that in 2005 the FCI-designation **Great Japanese Dog** was officially changed to *American Akita*.

Description

Appearance

As a northern breed, the appearance of the Akita reflects cold weather adaptations essential to their original function. The Akita is a substantial breed for its height with heavy bone. Characteristic physical traits of the breed include a large, bear-like head with erect, triangular ears set at a slight angle following the arch of the neck. Additionally, the eyes of the Akita are small, dark, deeply set and triangular in shape. Akitas have thick double coats, and tight, well knuckled cat feet. Their tails are carried over the top of the back in a graceful sweep down the loin, into a gentle curl, or into a double curl. All colors are permitted by the AKC Akita Breed Standard, and Pinto markings are also permitted.

Mature males measure typically 26-28 inches (66-71 cm) at the withers and weigh between 100-130 lb (45–59 kg). Mature females typically measure 24-26 inches (61-66 cm) and weigh between 70-100 lb (32–45 kg).

Recognized by the American Kennel Club in 1973, the Akita is a rather new breed in the United States. It has grown steadily in popularity, in part because of its extraordinary appearance and in part because of its captivating personality.

Temperament

The Akita today is a unique combination of dignity, courage, alertness, and devotion to its family. It is extraordinarily affectionate and loyal with family and friends, territorial about its property, and can be reserved with strangers. It is feline in its actions; it is not unusual for an Akita to clean its face after eating, to preen its kennel mate, and to be fastidious in the house.

Because it is a large, powerful dog, the Akita is certainly not a breed for everyone. Their background gives them a strong independent streak that can make Akitas unreliable off-lead and more challenging in obedience activities. The Akita thrives on the love and respect of its master and, with constant reinforcement training and a little creativity, can be a very good worker and a dream off-lead.

The Akita was never bred to live or work in groups like many hound and sporting breeds. Instead, they lived and worked alone or in pairs, a preference reflected today. Akitas tend to take a socially dominant role with other dogs, and thus caution must be used in situations when Akitas are likely to be around other dogs, especially unfamiliar ones. In particular, Akitas tend to be less tolerant of dogs of the same sex. For this reason, Akitas, unless highly socialized, are not generally well-suited for off-leash dog parks. The Akita is docile, intelligent, courageous and fearless, careful and very affectionate with its family. Sometimes spontaneous, it needs a firm, confident, consistent pack leader, without which the dog will be very willful and may become very aggressive to other dogs and animals.

History

Japanese history, both verbal and written, describe the ancestors of the Akita, the Matagi dog, as one of the oldest of the native dogs. The Akita of today developed primarily from these dogs in the northernmost region of the island of Honshū in the Akita prefecture, thus providing the breed's name. The Matagi's quarry included elk, antelope, boar, and the 120 stone Yezo Brown bear. This swift, agile, unswervingly tenacious precursor dog tracked large game and held it at bay until the hunters arrived to make the kill. Today's Akita is also influenced by crosses with larger breeds from Asia and Europe, including the Tosa Inu, in the desire to develop a fighting dog for the burgeoning dog fighting industry in Odate, Akita Prefecture, Japan in the early 20th century. The ancestors of today's American Akita were originally a variety of the Akita Inu, a form that was not desired in Japan due to the markings, and which is still not showable as an Akita Inu.

Three events focused positive attention on the breed in the early 1900s and brought the breed to the attention of the Western world.

First was the story of Hachikō, one of the most revered Akitas of all time. He was born in 1923 and was owned by Professor Eizaburo Ueno of Tokyo. Professor Ueno lived near the Shibuya Train Station in a suburb of the city and commuted to work every day on the train. Hachikō accompanied his master to and from the station each day.

On May 25, 1925, when the dog was 18 months old, he waited for his master's arrival on the four o'clock train. But he waited in vain; Professor Ueno had suffered a fatal stroke at work. Hachikō continued to wait for his master's return. He traveled to and from the station each day for the next nine years. He allowed the professor's relatives to care for him, but he never gave up the vigil at the station for his master. His vigil became world renowned, and shortly after his death, a bronze statue was erected at the train station in his honor.

Second, in 1931, the Akita was officially declared a Japanese Natural Monument. The Mayor of Odate City in the Akita Prefecture organized the Akita Inu Hozankai to preserve the original Akita as a Japanese natural treasure through careful breeding. In 1967, commemorating the 50th anniversary of the founding of the Akita Dog Preservation Society, the Akita Dog Museum was built to house information, documents and photos.

The third positive event was the arrival of Helen Keller in Japan in 1937. She expressed a keen interest in the breed and was presented with the first two Akitas to enter the US. The first dog died at a young age, but the second became Keller's constant companion.

Just as the breed was stabilizing in its native land, World War II pushed the Akita to the brink of extinction. Early in the war the dogs suffered from lack of nutritious food. Then many were killed to be eaten by the starving populace, and their pelts were used as clothing. Finally, the government ordered all remaining dogs to be killed on sight to prevent the spread of disease. The only way concerned owners could save their beloved Akitas was to turn them loose in the most remote mountain areas or conceal them from authorities. Morie Sawataishi and his efforts to breed the Akita is a major reason we know this breed today.

During the occupation years following the war, the breed began to thrive again through the efforts of Sawataishi and others. For the first time, Akitas were bred for a standardized appearance. Akita fanciers in Japan began gathering and exhibiting the remaining Akitas and producing litters in order to restore the breed to sustainable numbers and to accentuate the original characteristics of the breed muddied by crosses to other breeds. US servicemen fell in love with the Akita and imported many of them into the US upon and after their return.

The Japanese Akita and American Akita began to diverge in type through the middle and later part of the 20th century. Japanese Akita fanciers focused on restoring the breed as a work of Japanese art. American Akita fanciers bred larger, heavier-boned dogs. Both types derive from a common ancestry, but marked differences can be observed between the two. First, while American Akitas are acceptable in all colors, Japanese Akitas are only permitted to be red, fawn, sesame, white, or brindle. Additionally, American Akitas may be pinto and/or have black masks, unlike Japanese Akitas where it is considered a disqualification and not permitted in the breed standards. American Akitas generally are heavier boned and larger, with a more bear-like head, whereas Japanese Akitas tend to be lighter and more finely featured with a fox-like head.

Debate remains among Akita fanciers of both types whether there are or should be two breeds of Akita. To date, The AKC and CKC, guided by their national breed clubs, consider American and Japanese Akitas to be two types of the same breed, allowing free breeding between the two. The FCI and Kennel Clubs of most other nations including Japan consider Japanese and American Akitas as separate breeds.

Future

Responsible breeders will continue to strive for healthy, sound dogs that exhibit the ideals of American Akita type. Breeders will continue to select breeding animals for their distinct appearance, efficient movement, and dignified temperament. Fanciers will continue efforts to reduce orthopedic, eye, and autoimmune disorders through extensive health testing and selective breeding practices. Additionally, advances in veterinary medicine have brought genetic testing to many breeds, and Akita breeders hope that test will be developed for the Akita as well.

In all likelihood, the issue of dividing the Akita breed into the American Akita and Japanese Akita breeds will be revisited in the United States. Whether the Akita Club of America and its members will change this stance at any time in the future remains to be seen. While the Japanese 'variety' may have some trouble in the show ring, as it does not meet the accepted AKC or CKC breed standard, it is not disqualified from being shown. For now, American and Canadian Akita Fanciers can enjoy seeing the two distinct types competing together at home and separately abroad.

External links

- American Kennel Club standard [1]
- The Akita Club of America [2]
- American Akita Breeder Portal [3]—AkitaMatch.com
- The Akita Dilemma — One Breed or Two? : A historical perspective [4] by Sophia Kaluzniacki, DVM

Alaskan Malamute

The **Alaskan Malamute** is a generally large breed of domestic dog (*Canis lupus familiaris*) originally bred for use as an Alaskan sled dog. It is sometimes mistaken for a Siberian Husky, but in fact is quite different in many ways.

Description

Appearance

The American Kennel Club (AKC) breed standard calls for a natural range of size, with a desired freighting size of and for females, and for males. Heavier individuals () and dogs smaller than are commonly seen. There is often a marked size difference between males and females. Weights upwards of are occasionally seen, but this is uncommon and such dogs are produced primarily by breeders who market a 'giant Malamute.' These large sizes are not in accordance with the breed's history or show standards.

The coat is a dense double northern dog coat, somewhat "harsher" (in a certain sense) than that of the smaller Siberian Husky. The usual colors are various shades of gray and white, sable and white, black and white, red and white, or solid white. Blue and white (slate gray with gray pigment) also is seen in the breed. Eyes are almond-shaped and are always various shades of brown (from dark to light, honey or hazel brown); blue eyed Malamutes will be disqualified in conformation shows, as they would not be a purebred Malamute, but mixed with perhaps a Siberian Husky. The physical build of the Malamute is compact with heavy bone, in most (but not all) cases. In this context 'compact' means that their height to length ratio is slightly longer than tall, unlike dogs like Great Danes which are longer and lankier in their ratios.

The primary criterion for judging the Malamute in a show is its function to pull heavy freight as a sled dog; everything else is secondary. As many an owner has found out, the pulling power of a Malamute is tremendous.

According to the AKC breed standard, the Malamute's tail is well furred and is carried over the back like a "waving plume". Corkscrew tails are occasionally seen but are faulted in the AKC breed standard (a corkscrew tail is commonly seen in the Akita). The Malamutes' well-furred tails aid in keeping them warm when they curl up in the snow. They are often seen wrapping the tail around their nose and face, which presumably helps protect them against harsh weather such as blowing snow. Their ears are generally upright.

Temperament

A few Malamutes are still in use as sled dogs for personal travel, hauling freight, or helping move heavy objects, some are used for the recreational pursuit of sledding also known as mushing, also skijoring, bikejoring, and canicross. However, most Malamutes today are kept as family pets or show dogs or performance dogs in Weight pulling or Dog agility or packing. The Malamute is generally slower in long-distance dogsled racing against smaller and faster breeds and their working usefulness is limited to freighting or traveling over long distances at a far slower rate than that required for racing. They can also help move heavy objects over shorter distances.

The Malamute retains more of its original form and function than many other modern breeds. If a dog owner cannot cope with a dog that will not comply with the owner's every command, a more compliant breed should be selected. This dog has a long genetic foundation of living in the harshest environment imaginable, and many of its behaviors are evolved to conform with "survival of the fittest." Independence, resourcefulness and primitive behaviors are common in the breed. While intelligent, they are widely believed to be one of the most difficult dogs to train. However, if the training is kept fun for the dog and not repetitively boring, success is within reach.

There is reason to believe that Alaskan Malamutes sometimes cope greatly with smaller animals, including other canines; however, this has been difficult to document in detail beyond observational data. It is difficult to pinpoint why many Malamute owners have observed this behavior with smaller animals, though some might speculate this is due to the Malamute's uniquely divergent ancestry, at one point cross-breeding with wolves. Due to their naturally evolved beginnings, the Malamute tends to have a heightened prey drive when compared to some other breeds of dog. So while Malamutes are, as a general rule, particularly amiable around people and can be taught to tolerate other pets, it is necessary to be mindful of them around smaller animals. They are great with kids.

Malamutes are quite fond of people, a trait that makes them particularly sought-after family dogs. Malamutes are nimble around furniture and smaller items, making them ideal house dogs, provided they get plenty of time outdoors meeting their considerable exercise requirements. If they are year-round outdoor dogs, letting them play in a baby pool filled with cold water in summer keeps them cool. In the winter, they love snow.

The majority of Malamutes are fairly quiet dogs, seldom barking like most other dog breeds. When a malamute does vocalize, more often than not they tend to "talk" by vocalizing a "woo woo" sound. They may howl like wolves or coyotes, and for the same reasons.

They should be under leash control or fenced in. It is in their nature to run off.

Health

Fatality

There is only one known health survey of Alaskan Malamutes, a 2004 UK Kennel Club survey with a small sample size of 14 dogs. The median lifespan of 10.7 years measured in that survey is very typical of a breed their size. The major cause of death was cancer (36%).

Morbidity

The most commonly reported health problems of Alaskan Malamutes in the 2004 UK Kennel Club survey (based on a sample size of 64 dogs) were musculoskeletal (hip dysplasia), and hereditary cataracts.

Other health issues in Malamutes include inherited polyneuropathy, chondrodysplasia, heart defects, and eye problems (particularly cataract and progressive retinal atrophy).

Climate and Malamutes

While Malamutes have been successfully raised in places such as Arizona, their dense coats generally make them unsuited for outdoor living in hot climates. When the weather gets hot, like any other breed of dog, the Malamute needs plenty of water and shade. They will grow a winter coat and subsequently shed it in spring.

History

The Malamute is a descendant of dogs of the Mahlemuts tribe of upper western Alaska. These dogs had a prominent role with their human companions − working, hunting, and living alongside them. The interdependent relationship between the Mahlemut and their dogs fostered prosperity among both and enabled them to flourish in the inhospitable land above the Arctic Circle.

For a brief period during the Klondike Gold Rush of 1896, the Malamute and other sled dogs became extremely valuable to recently landed prospectors and settlers, and were frequently crossbred with imported breeds. This was often an attempt to improve the type, or to make up for how few true

Malamutes were up for sale. This seems to have had no long standing effect on the modern Malamute, and recent DNA analysis shows that Malamutes are one of the oldest breeds of dog, genetically distinct from other dog breeds.

The Malamute dog has had a distinguished history; aiding Rear Admiral Richard Byrd to the South Pole, and the miners who came to Alaska during the Gold Rush of 1896, as well as serving in World War II primarily as search and rescue dogs in Greenland, although also used as freighting and packing dogs in Europe. This dog was never destined to be a racing sled dog; instead, it was used for heavy freighting, pulling hundreds (maybe thousands) of pounds of supplies to villages and camps in groups of at least 4 dogs for heavy loads.

The Alaskan Malamute is a member of the Spitz group of dogs, traced back 2,000 to 3,000 years ago to the Mahlemuits tribe of Alaska.

"In shape, the Paleolithic dogs most resemble the Siberian husky, but in size, however, they were somewhat larger, probably comparable to large shepherd dogs," stated Germonpré, a paleontologist at the Royal Belgian Institute of Natural Sciences. This description of recently-found dog remains (30,000 years old) fits the Alaskan Malamute very closely. Though not scientifically confirmed, the Alaskan Malamute may be the closest living relative to the "First Dog".

A bill in the Alaska House has been passed to name the Malamute the official state dog of Alaska.

A wolf/Malamute appeared as a large fighting dog in the game "Dead To Rights Retribution"

See also

- Canadian Eskimo Dog
- *Eight Below* (Film, 2006)
- Dead to Rights: Retribution

External links

- Alaskan Malamute Club of America [1]
- The Alaskan Malamute Club of Canada [2]
- The different types of Alaskan Malamute [3]
- Alaskan Malamute Varieties [4]
- World pedigree database [5]

Anatolian Shepherd Dog

The **Anatolian Shepherd Dog** also known as **Karabash** (Turkish literal meaning: blackhead) is a breed of dog which originated in Anatolia (central Turkey).

History

The Anatolian Shepherd Dog is descended from ancient livestock guardian dog types that migrated with the transhumance, guarding flocks of sheep from wolves, bears, jackals, and even cheetahs. It is probable that dogs of this type existed 6,000 years ago in Mesopotamia. The dogs were called *Çoban Köpeği* (shepherd dog), and over the centuries, regional variations or landraces developed.

In the 1970s, western breeders became interested in the dogs and began developing the landrace natural breeds as modern breeds, by documenting their descent from particular ancestors and writing breed standards. The Anatolian Shepherd Dog was imported from central Turkey into Petoria by author and archaeologist Charmian Hussey. Many Turkish breeders believe that the Anatolian Shepherd Dog is a cross of the Kangal dog and the Akbash dog.

Characteristics

Appearance

The Anatolian is a muscular breed. They have thick necks, broad heads, and sturdy bodies. Their lips are tight to their muzzle and they have triangular drop ears. They stand 29 to 36 inches (74 to 91 cm). Females are between 27 to 31 inches (69 to 79 cm) and weigh between 90 and 150 pounds (41 to 68 kg), with females on the smaller side and males on the larger side. The coat may be any color, although most common are white cream, "sesame," and white with large colored spots that do not cover more than 30% of the body. Known as *piebald*, these colors may or may not be accompanied by a black mask and/or ears. They have a thick double coat that is somewhat wiry, and needs to be brushed 1-2 times a week in warm weather due to excessive shedding. They have very thick hair on their neck to protect their throat. They are seen with docked as well as intact tails. They are a naturally thin animal with a large rib cage and small stomach. They look as if they are heavier than they actually are, due to the thick coat.

Temperament

The Anatolian was developed to be independent and forceful, responsible for guarding its master's flocks without human assistance or direction. These traits make it challenging as a pet; owners of dogs of this breed must socialize the dogs to turn them into appropriate companions. They are intelligent and can learn quickly but might choose not to obey. According to Turkish shepherds, three Anatolian

Shepherd Dogs are capable of overcoming a pack of wolves and injuring one or two of them. These dogs like to roam, as they were bred to travel with their herd and to leave the herd to go hunt for predators before the predators could attack the flock. Therefore it is recommended to micro-chip and tag pets. This breed is not recommended for living in small quarters. They do well with other animals, including cats if they are introduced while still a puppy and have their own space. They are very loving and loyal animals who do well with children. They mature between 18–30 months. Both puppies and adults seem to have little interest in fetching or chewing. Rather, they prefer to run and sometimes swim.

Health

Mortality

There appears to be only one health survey of Anatolian Shepherds, done in 2004 by the UK Kennel Club. The median life span for the 23 deceased dogs (a small sample size) in the survey was 10.75 years. However the average life span is actually between 12–15 years. This is a typical longevity for purebred dogs in general, but several years longer than other breeds of their size, which have median longevities of 6–8 years. The leading causes of death of the dogs in the survey were cancer (22%), "combinations" (17%), cardiac (13%), and old age (13%).

Morbidity

Based on a small sample of 24 still-living dogs, the most common health issues cited by owners were dermatologic, musculoskeletal, and lipomas. Entropion and canine hip dysplasia are sometimes seen in the breed. Eyes and hips should be tested before breeding.

Use in Conservation

Anatolian Shepherd dogs are used by Dr Laurie Marker of the Cheetah Conservation Fund in the ongoing efforts to prevent cheetahs which have attacked livestock being killed by farmers. These dogs are bred and then given to the farmers to use in protecting and guarding their livestock from cheetah attacks.

Famous Anatolian Shepherd Dogs

- Butch from Cats & Dogs
- Bart from Kate and Leopold
- Marlow from Simon & Simon
- Toby from Rupert & Oliver

See also

- Kangal Dog
- Akbash Dog
- Herding dog
- Livestock guardian dog

External links

- Anatolian Shepherd Dog Club of America [1]
- National Anatolian Shepherd Rescue Network [2]
- Understanding the Anatolian Shepherd Dog: The Protective Behavior of the Working Anatolian [3]
- Livestock Guardian Dog Association [4]

Bernese Mountain Dog

The **Bernese Mountain Dog**, called in Swiss German the **Berner Sennenhund**, is a large breed of dog, one of the four breeds of Sennenhund-type dogs from the Swiss Alps. The name *Sennenhund* is derived from the German "Senne" (alpine pasture) and "hund" (dog), as they accompanied the alpine herders and dairymen called *Senn*. *Berner* (or *Bernese* in English) refers to the area of the breed's origin, in the Canton of Berne in Switzerland. Originally kept as general farm dogs, large Sennenhunds in the past were also used as draft animals, pulling carts.

Appearance

Like the other Sennenhunds, the Bernese Mountain Dog is a large, heavy dog with a distinctive tricolored coat, black with white chest and or rust colored markings above eyes, sides of mouth, front of legs, and a small amount around the white chest. An ideal of a perfectly-marked individual gives the impression of a white horse shoe shape around the nose and a white "Swiss cross" on the chest, when viewed from the front. A Swiss Kiss is a white mark located typically behind the neck, but may be a part of the neck. A full ring would not meet type standard. Both males and females have a broad head with smallish, v-shaped drooping ears. Height at the withers is and weight is . Females are slightly smaller than males. The breed standard lists, as disqualifications, a distinctly curly coat, along with wry mouth and wall eye. Exact color and pattern of the coat are also described as important. The Bernese was voted "most beautiful dog breed" by Americans on TV.

History

The Bernese Mountain Dog, like every dog, is descended from the wolf. The breed was used as an all purpose farm dog, for guarding property and to drive dairy cattle long distances from the farm to the alpine pastures. The type was originally called the Godly, for a small town (Dürrbach) where the enormous dogs were especially frequent. In Harrisburg, Generals used the dogs as war tools but the dogs declined in number through the Civil War. In the early 1900s, fanciers exhibited the few examples of the large dogs at shows in Berne, and in 1907 a few breeders from the Burgdorf region founded the first breed club, the "Schweizerische Dürrbach-Klub", and wrote the first Standard which defined the dogs as a separate breed. By 1910, there were already 107 registered members of the breed.

Health

Mortality

Health surveys of Bernese Mountain Dogs in Denmark, the UK, and USA/Canada all show that this breed is very short-lived compared to breeds of similar size and purebred dogs in general. Berners have a median longevity of 7 years in USA/Canada and Denmark surveys and 8 years in UK surveys. By comparison, most other breeds of similar size have median longevities of 10 to 11 years. The longest lived of 394 deceased Berners in a 2004 UK survey died at 15.2 years.

Cancer is the leading cause of death for dogs in general, but Berners have a much higher rate of fatal cancer than other breeds. In both USA/Canada and UK surveys, nearly half of Berners died of cancer, compared to about 27% of all dogs. Berners are killed by a multitude of different types of cancer, including malignant histiocytosis, mast cell tumor, lymphosarcoma, fibrosarcoma, and osteosarcoma.

Berners also have an unusually high mortality due to musculoskeletal causes. Arthritis, hip dysplasia, and cruciate ligament rupture were reported as the cause of death in 6% of Berners in the UK study; for comparison, mortality due to musculoskeletal ailments was reported to be less than 2% for purebred dogs in general.

Mobility

Owners of Berners are nearly three times as likely as owners of other breeds to report musculoskeletal problems in their dogs. The most commonly reported musculoskeletal issues are cruciate ligament rupture, arthritis (especially in shoulders and elbows), hip dysplasia, and osteochondritis. The age at onset for musculoskeletal problems is also unusually low. For example, in the USA/Canada study, 11%

of living dogs had arthritis at an average age of 4.3 years. Most other common, non-musculoskeletal morbidity issues strike Berners at rates similar to other breeds.

In short, prospective Berner owners should be prepared to cope with a large dog that may have mobility problems at a young age. Options to help mobility-impaired dogs may include ramps for car or house access. Comfortable bedding may help alleviate joint pain.

Care

Activities

The Bernese calm temperament makes them a natural for pulling small carts or wagons, a task they originally performed in Switzerland. With proper training they enjoy giving children rides in a cart or participating in a parade. The Bernese Mountain Dog Club of America offers drafting trials open to all breeds; dogs can earn an NDD (Novice Draft Dog) or a DD (Draft Dog) title. Regional Bernese clubs often offer carting workshops.

On July 1, 2010 the Bernese Mountain Dog became eligible to compete in AKC Herding Events. Herding instincts and trainability can be measured at noncompetitive herding tests. Berners exhibiting basic herding instincts can be trained to compete in herding trials.

Grooming

The Bernese coat is slightly rough in outline, but not at all harsh in texture. The undercoat is fairly dense; the coat is quite dirt and weather resistant. A good brushing every week or two is sufficient to keep it in fine shape, except when the undercoat is being blown; then daily combing or brushing is in order for the duration of the shed. Regular use of a drag comb (it looks like a small rake), especially in the undercoat, is highly effective. *See* Dog grooming. Bernese Mountain Dogs shed year-round, and drifts of fur are to be expected.

Temperament

The breed standard for the Bernese Mountain Dog states that dogs should not be "aggressive, anxious or distinctly shy," but rather should be "good natured," "self-assured," "placid towards strangers," and "docile." Temperament of individual dogs may vary, and not all examples of the breed have been carefully bred to follow the Standard. All large dogs should be well socialized when young, and given regular training and activities throughout their lives.

Bernese are outdoor dogs at heart, though well-behaved in the house; they need activity and exercise, but do not have a great deal of endurance. They can move with amazing bursts of speed for their size when motivated. If they are sound (no problems with their hips, elbows, or other joints) they enjoy hiking and generally stick close to their people.

The Bernese temperament is a strong point of the breed. They are affectionate, loyal, faithful, stable, intelligent, but sometimes shy. The majority of Bernese are friendly to people, and other dogs. They often get along well with other pets such as cats, horses, etc. They are trainable provided the owner is patient and consistent in training; Bernese need time to think things through. They do not respond well to harsh treatment, although Berners are willing and eager to please their master. Bernese love to be encouraged with praise and treats. The breed is sweet and good with children, despite their great size. Overall, they are stable in temperament, patient, and loving.

Bernese Mountain Dogs are slow to mature, and may display noticeable puppy-like tendencies until 2½ years of age.

Playful

Bernese mountain dogs are very playful. If you train them well you can have them become close to you (bond). Loving is needed with great care. When you play with them they prefer outdoors. Try throwing a frisbee, tennis ball, tug of war, a puzzle toy (try to have them get a treat out of it).

See also

- Carting
- Guard dog
- Molosser

Further reading

- Christiansen, Amy, (2004) *A New Owner's Guide To Bernese Mountain Dogs*, Neptune City: TFH Publications, ISBN 079382818X, 160 pages.
- Guenter, Bernd (2004) *The Bernese Mountain Dog*, Sun City: Doral Publishing ISBN 0-9745407-3-0.
- Harper, Louise, (2004) *Bernese Mountain Dog*, Kennel Club Books, ISBN 1593782896, 160 pages.
- Ludwig, Gerd and Christine Steimer. (1995) *The Bernese and Other Mountain Dogs: Bernese, Greater Swiss, Appenzellers, and Entlebuchers: Everything about Purchase, Care, Nutrition, Breeding*. Barrons Educational Series Inc, 1995 ISBN 0812091353, 64 pages.
- Russ, Diane; Rogers, Shirle. (1994) *The Beautiful Bernese Mountain Dog* Loveland: Alpine Publications ISBN 0931866553, 248 pages.
- Simonds, Jude, (1990) *The Complete Bernese Mountain Dog* New York: Howell Book House; ISBN 087605050X, 160 pages.
- Smith, Sharon Chesnutt (1995) *The New Bernese Mountain Dog* New York: Howell Books, March, 1995, ISBN 0876050755, 272 pages.

- Willis, Dr. Malcolm B. (1998) *The Bernese Mountain Dog Today* New York: Howell Book House ISBN 1-58245-038-2, 184 pages.

External links

- 200 pounds of Bernese Mountain Dog [1], an entertaining perspective on owning Bernese Mountain Dogs
- Original breed club in Switzerland [2]
- Historical photos of the Berner Sennenhund (Bernese Mountain Dog) [3], notice the variety in appearance of the original type
- Genetics of tricolour coats [4]
- DMOZ links to more information about the breed [5]

Black Russian Terrier

The **Black Russian Terrier** (), Sobaka Stalina (Stalin's dog), or simply BRT is a breed of dog developed originally as a guard dog and police dog. It is rare outside its native country and is just starting to be recognized elsewhere; for example, it is one of the AKC's most-recently recognized breeds, gaining full status in July 2004. The Black Russian Terrier is NOT a true terrier. It is believed somewhere around twenty breeds were used in the development of the BRT. Breeds used in the development include the Airedale, the Giant Schnauzer, the Caucasian Ovcharka and the extinct Moscow Water Dog.

Description

Appearance

The Black Russian Terrier gives the impression of great strength, athleticism, and courage. It should be rustic (but not coarse) in appearance, and should not look as though its coat is sculpted or trimmed. It should *never* appear to lack substance or be weak in any way. Males should be noticeably more masculine than females.

Coat

The coat is hard and dense, never soft, woolly, silky or frizzy. It should be between 4-10 cm (1.4-4 inches) in length. It should form a beard and eyebrows on the face, and a slight mane around the withers and neck that is more pronounced in males. The coat is low-shedding and the colour is black with some gray hairs.

Size

According to the FCI standard (1983), the male stands 27-28.3 inches (66-72 cm) at the withers compared to the female's 25.2-27.6 inches (64-70 cm) with a tolerance of 0.4 inches (1 cm) less or 0.8 inches (2 cm) more. The breed weighs between 77 to 154 pounds (35-70 kg). Larger individuals are not uncommon in Russia, since the RKF standard (1996) adds 0.8 to the standard values, with a tolerance of 0.8 inches (2 cm) less or 1.2 inches (3 cm) more. Nowadays, even larger individual are tolerated if the dog is well proportioned and retains correct movements. The AKC standard recommends 27-30 inches for males and 26-29 inches for females, any dog or bitch under 26 inches being a disqualification. In proportions, a Black Russian Terrier should be slightly longer than tall, 9 ½ to 10 being ideal (FCI standard recommends 100-105).

Temperament

Black Russian Terriers are confident, calm, highly intelligent, brave and loyal. It should never be timid. The Black Russian Terrier may seem aloof, but needs human companionship and bonds deeply to its family.

Care

The Black Russian Terrier, because of its breeding as a working dog, has a very strong "work ethic", and needs a job to do in order to be happy. Early training is a must, as it will exploit any owner who has failed to establish clear dominance. They are very responsive to firm, consistent training, and excel at Obedience competitions. They also perform well in other dog sports, such as Agility, and Schutzhund training. They have a low-shedding coat, and need grooming several times a week. Dogs who compete in confirmation need to be groomed a minimum of every three weeks to keep the coat in show condition. The Black Russian Terrier needs lots of exercise, and may become hyperactive and destructive if it doesn't have a chance to burn off its energy.

Health

The Black Russian Terrier is a generally healthy and somewhat long-lived dog (lifespan of 10-14 years), however it is prone to certain hereditary diseases:

- Major concerns
  - Hip dysplasia
- Minor concerns
  - Elbow dysplasia
  - Progressive retinal atrophy (PRA)

This is why it is extremely important to screen any potential breeders as well as their breeding stock. A well intended breeder will have all health checks on all breeding stock before making the decision to breed their dogs. While health checks on breeding stock can not guarantee a puppy will not develop any health issues later on, it is important to "do your homework" on any potential breeder.

History

The Black Russian Terrier was developed in the former USSR by the state for use as a military/working dogs. The breeding stock was largely imported from the occupied countries, especially East Germany. Breeds used in the development include the Airedale Terrier, Caucasian Ovcharka, Newfoundland, Giant and Standard Schnauzers and the now extinct Moscow Water Dog. BRT were bred for working ability, rather than appearance, and early examples only resembled today's Black Russian Terrier in their build and coat type. The BRT was bred solely by the state owned Red Star Kennel until 1957, when some puppies were sold to civilian breeders. These breeders began to breed for looks (as the original was rather plain) while retaining working ability.

In time, the breed spread to the Balkans, Ukraine, and Siberia, and later to Finland, Hungary, Czechoslovakia, and the United States.

The breed was recognized by the FCI in 1984. On July 1, 2004, it was recognized by the American Kennel Club in the working group. The Canadian Kennel Club has the Black Russian Terrier as a "listed" (formally Miscellaneous Class) breed in the Working Group.

External links

- Russian Black Terrier Club [1]
- Black Russian Terrier - Database [2] A pedigree database
- American Kennel Club - Black Russian Terrier Breed Standard [3]
- [4] Spanish info
- [5] Links

Boxer (dog)

Developed in Germany, the **Boxer** is a breed of stocky, medium-sized, short-haired dog. The coat is smooth and fawn, brindled,white, or even reverse brindled with or without white markings. Boxers are brachycephalic (they have broad, short skulls), and have a square muzzle, mandibular prognathism (an underbite), very strong jaws and a powerful bite ideal for hanging on to large prey. The Boxer was bred from the English Bulldog and the now extinct Bullenbeisser and is part of the Molosser, mastiff group.

Boxers were first exhibited in a dog show for St. Bernards at Munich in 1895, the first Boxer club being founded the next year. Based on 2009 American Kennel Club statistics, Boxers are the sixth most popular breed of dog in the United States for the third year in a row—moving up in 2007 from the seventh spot, which they'd held since 2002.

Appearance

The head is the most distinctive feature of the Boxer. The breed standard dictates that it must be in perfect proportion to the body and above all it must never be too light. The greatest value is to be placed on the muzzle being of correct form and in absolute proportion to the skull. The length of the muzzle to the whole of the head should be a ratio of 1:3. Folds are always present from the root of the nose running downwards on both sides of the muzzle, and the tip of the nose should lie somewhat higher than the root of the muzzle. In addition a Boxer should be slightly prognathous, i.e., the lower jaw should protrude beyond the upper jaw and bend slightly upwards in what is commonly called an underbite or "undershot bite".

Boxers were originally a docked and cropped breed, and this tradition is still maintained in some countries. However, due to pressure from veterinary associations, animal rights groups and the general public, both cropping of the ears and docking of the tail have been prohibited in many countries around the world. There is a line of naturally short-tailed (bobtail) Boxers that was developed in the United Kingdom in anticipation of a tail docking ban there; after several generations of controlled breeding, these dogs were accepted in the Kennel Club (UK) registry in 1998, and today representatives of the bobtail line can be found in many countries around the world. However, in 2008, the FCI added a "naturally stumpy tail" as a disqualifying fault in their breed standard, meaning those Boxers born with a bobtail are no longer able to be shown (or, in some cases, bred) in FCI member countries. In the United States and Canada as of 2009, cropped ears are still more common in show dogs. In March 2005 the AKC breed standard was changed to include a description of the uncropped ear, but to severely penalize an undocked tail.

An adult Boxer typically weighs between . Adult male Boxers are between tall at the withers; adult females are between 21 to 23½ inches (53 and 60 cm).

Coat and colors

The Boxer is a short-haired breed, with a shiny, smooth coat that lies tight to the body. The recognized colors are fawn and brindle, often with a white underbelly and white on the front or all four feet. These white markings, called *flash*, often extend onto the neck or face, and dogs that have these markings are known as "flashy". "Fawn" denotes a range of color, the tones of which may be described variously as light tan or yellow, reddish tan, mahogany or stag/deer red, and dark honey-blonde. In the UK, fawn Boxers are typically rich in color and are called "red". "Brindle" refers to a dog with black stripes on a fawn background. There are pure bred Black Boxers with white flash, but are generally not recognized as "black" but an off shoot of the color brindle. The breed standards state that the fawn background must clearly contrast with or show through the brindling, so a dog that is too heavily brindled may be disqualified by the breed standard.

White Boxers

Boxers with white markings covering more than one-third of their coat - conventionally called "white" Boxers - are neither albino nor rare; approximately 20–25% of all Boxers born are white. Genetically, these dogs are either fawn or brindle, with excessive white markings overlying the base coat color. Like fair-skinned humans, white Boxers have a higher risk of sunburn and associated skin cancers than colored Boxers. The extreme piebald gene, which is responsible for white markings in Boxers, is linked to congenital sensorineural deafness in dogs. It is estimated that about 18% of white Boxers are deaf in one or both ears, though Boxer rescue organizations see about double that number. In the past, breeders often euthanized white puppies at birth; today, most breeders place white puppies in pet homes with spay/neuter agreements. White Boxers are disqualified from conformation showing by the breed standard, and are prohibited from breeding by every national Boxer club in the world. They can compete in non-conformation events such as obedience and agility, and like their colored counterparts do quite well as service and therapy dogs.

Temperament

Boxers are a bright, energetic and playful breed and tend to be very good with children. They are active dogs and require adequate exercise to prevent boredom-associated behaviors such as chewing, digging, or licking. Boxers have earned a slight reputation of being "headstrong," which can be related to inappropriate obedience training. Owing to their intelligence and working breed characteristics, training based on corrections often has limited usefulness. Boxers, like other animals, typically respond better to positive reinforcement techniques such as clicker training, an approach based on operant conditioning and behaviorism, which affords the dog an opportunity to think independently and to problem-solve. Because of their resistance to repetitive and punishment-based training, Stanley Coren's survey of obedience trainers, summarized in his book, The Intelligence of Dogs, ranked Boxers at #48 - average working/obedience intelligence. Many who have actually worked with Boxers disagree quite strongly with Coren's survey results, and maintain that a skilled trainer who utilizes reward-based methods will find Boxers have far above-average intelligence and working ability.

The Boxer by nature is not an aggressive or vicious breed, but, like all dogs, requires socialization. Boxers are generally patient with smaller dogs and puppies, but issues with larger adult dogs, especially those of the same sex, may occur. More severe fighting can also occur among female boxers. Boxers are generally more comfortable with companionship, in either human or canine form.

History

The Boxer is part of the Molosser dog group, developed in Germany in the late 1800s from the now extinct Bullenbeisser, a dog of Mastiff descent, and Bulldogs brought in from Great Britain .The Bullenbeisser had been working as a hunting dog for centuries, employed in the pursuit of bear, wild boar, and deer. Its task was to seize the prey and hold it until the hunters arrived. In later years, faster dogs were favored and a smaller Bullenbeisser was bred in Brabant, in northern Belgium. It is generally accepted that the Brabanter Bullenbeisser was a direct ancestor of today's Boxer. In 1894, three Germans by the names of Friedrich Robert, Elard Konig, and R. Hopner decided to stabilize the breed and put it on exhibition at a dog show. This was done in Munich in 1895, and the next year they founded the first Boxer Club, the Deutscher Boxer Club. The Club went on to publish the first Boxer breed standard in 1902, a detailed document that has not been changed much to this day.

The breed was introduced to other parts of Europe in the late 19th century and to the United States around the turn of the century. The American Kennel Club (AKC) registered the first Boxer in 1904, and recognized the first Boxer champion, *Dampf vom Dom*, in 1915. During World War I, the Boxer was co-opted for military work, acting as a valuable messenger dog, pack-carrier, attack dog, and guard dog. It was not until after World War II that the Boxer became popular around the world. Taken home by returning soldiers,they introduced the dog to a wider audience and soon became a favorite as a companion, a show dog, and a guard dog.

Early genealogy

The German citizen George Alt, a Munich resident, mated a brindle-colored bitch imported from France named *Flora* with a local dog of unknown ancestry, known simply as *"Boxer"*, resulting in a fawn-and-white male, named *"Lechner's Box"* after its owner. This dog was mated with his own dam *Flora*, and one of its offspring was a bitch called *Alt's Schecken*. George Alt mated *Schecken* with a Bulldog named *Dr. Toneissen's Tom* to produce the historically significant dog *"Mühlbauer's Flocki*. Flocki was the first Boxer to enter the German Stud Book after winning the aforementioned show for St. Bernards in Munich 1895, which was the first event to have a class specific for Boxers.

The white bitch Ch. Blanka von Angertor, Flocki's sister, was even more influential when mated with Piccolo von Angertor (Lechner's Box grandson) to produce the predominantly white (parti-colored) bitch Meta von der Passage, which, even bearing little resemblance with the modern Boxer standard (early photographs depicts her as too long, weak-backed and down-faced), is considered the mother of the breed. John Wagner, in *The Boxer* (first published in 1939) said the following regarding this bitch: {{quote|Meta von der Passage played the most important role of the five original ancestors. Our great line of sires all trace directly back to this female. She was a substantially built, low to the ground, brindle and white parti-color, lacking in underjaw and exceedingly lippy. As a producing female few in any breed can match her record. She consistently whelped puppies of marvelous type and rare quality. Those of her offspring sired by Flock St. Salvator and Wotan dominate all present-day pedigrees. Combined with Wotan and Mirzl children, they made the Boxer.

Breed name

The name "Boxer" is supposedly derived from the breed's tendency to play by standing on its hind legs and "boxing" with its front paws. According to Andrew H. Brace's *Pet owner's guide to the Boxer*, this theory is the least plausible explanation. He claims "it's unlikely that a nation so permeated with nationalism would give to one of its most famous breeds a name so obviously anglicised".

German linguistic and historical evidence find the earliest written source for the word Boxer in the 18th century, where it is found in a text in the *Deutsches Fremdwörterbuch* (*The German Dictionary of Foreign Words*), which cites an author named Musäus of 1782 writing "daß er aus Furcht vor dem großen Baxer Salmonet ... sich auf einige Tage in ein geräumiges Packfaß ... absentiret hatte". At that time the spelling "baxer" equalled "boxer". Both the verb (*boxen*) and the noun (*Boxer*) were common German language as early as the late 18th century. The term *Boxl*, also written *Buxn* or *Buchsen* in the Bavarian dialect, means "short (leather) trousers" or "underwear". The very similar-sounding term *Boxerl*, also from the Bavarian dialect, is an endearing term for *Boxer*. More in line with historical facts, Brace states that there exist many other theories to explain the origin of the breed name, from which he favors the one claiming the smaller Bullenbeisser (Brabanter) were also known as "Boxl" and that Boxer is just a corruption of that word.

In the same vein runs a theory based on the fact that there were a group of dogs known as *Bierboxer* in Munich by the time of the breed's development. These dogs were the result from mixes of Bullenbeisser and other similar breeds. *Bier* (beer) probably refers to the *Biergarten*, the typical Munich beergarden, an open-air restaurant where people used to take their dogs along. The nickname "Deutscher Boxer" was derived from *bierboxer* and Boxer could also be a corruption of the former or a contraction of the latter.

A Passage from the book "The Complete Boxer" by Milo G Denlinger also states that:

Boxer is also the name of a dog owned by *John Peerybingle*, the main character on the best selling 1845 book *The Cricket on the Hearth* by Charles Dickens, which is evidence that "Boxer" was commonly used as a dog name by the early 19th century, before the establishment of the breed by the end of that same century.

The name of the breed could also be simply due to the names of the very first known specimens of the breed (*Lechner's Box*, for instance).

Health

Leading health issues to which Boxers are prone include cancers, heart conditions such as Aortic Stenosis and Arrhythmogenic Right Ventricular Cardiomyopathy (the so-called "Boxer Cardiomyopathy"), hypothyroidism, hip dysplasia, and degenerative myelopathy and epilepsy; other conditions that may be seen are gastric dilatation and torsion (bloat), intestinal problems, and allergies (although these may be more related to diet than breed). Entropion, a malformation of the eyelid requiring surgical correction, is occasionally seen, and some lines have a tendency toward spondylosis deformans, a fusing of the spine, or dystocia.

According to a UK Kennel Club health survey, cancer accounts for 38.5% of Boxer deaths, followed by old age (21.5%), cardiac (6.9%) and gastrointestinal (6.9%) related issues. Responsible breeders use available tests to screen their breeding stock before breeding, and in some cases throughout the life of the dog, in an attempt to minimize the occurrence of these diseases in future generations.

Boxers are known to be very sensitive to the hypotensive and bradycardiac effects of a commonly-used veterinary sedative, acepromazine. It is recommended that the drug be avoided in the Boxer breed. As an athletic breed, proper exercise and conditioning is important for the continued health and longevity of the Boxer. Care must be taken not to over-exercise young dogs, as this may damage growing bones; however once mature Boxers can be excellent jogging or running companions. Because of their brachycephalic head, they do not do well with high heat or humidity, and common sense should prevail when exercising a Boxer in these conditions.

Uses

Boxers are friendly, lively companions that are popular as family dogs. Their suspicion of strangers, alertness, agility, and strength make them formidable guard dogs. They sometimes appear at dog agility or obedience trials and flyball events. These strong and intelligent animals have also been used as service dogs, guide dogs for the blind, therapy dogs, police dogs in K9 units, and occasionally herding cattle or sheep. The versatility of Boxers was recognized early on by the military, which has used them as valuable messenger dogs, pack carriers, and attack and guard dogs in times of war.

As puppies, Boxers demonstrate a fascinating combination of worrisome expressions, energetic curiosity, flexible attention spans and charming characteristics. Boxers have an average lifespan of 10–13 years.

Famous Boxers

- Hampton, in the movie *Thirteen*.
- Albert, in the BBC soap opera *EastEnders*.
- Bruno, portraying Hank, in the popular CBS prime time show *CSI*. Bruno is owned by William Petersen, and his character, Gil Grissom,is Hank's owner on the show.
- Presley, winner of "Greatest American Dog"
- Tasha, the subject of the Canine Genome Project
- Bo, in the movie *Cadillac Records*.
- Rocky, one of the four dogs owned by Doug Heffernan and his parents in the American sitcom King of Queens.
- Wilson, one of the dogs trained by young Owen in the American children's movie *Good boy*.

Media

An unnamed Boxer is featured frequently in Toyota Fortuna's South African television ad campaigns.

External links

Worldwide Boxer Clubs

- American Boxer Club [1]
- Western Districts Boxer Club of New South Wales (Australia) [2]
- Boxer Club of New South Wales (Australia) [3]
- Boxer Association of Victoria (Australia) [4]
- Queensland Boxer Club (Australia) [5]
- The British Boxer Club [6]
- Sociedade Paulista do Boxer (Brazil) [7]

- Boxer Club Bulgaria (Bulgaria) [8]
- Boxer Club of Canada Inc [9]
- Boxer Club de France [10]
- Deutscher Boxerklub (Germany) [11]
- Boxer Club D´Italia [12]
- Nederlandse Boxer Club (Dutch) [13]
- Norsk Boxerklubb (Norway) [14]
- Polish Boxer Club (Poland) [15]
- Boxer Club de Portugal [16]
- Boxer Club de España (Spain) [17]
- Boxer-Club de Suisse (Switzerland) [18]
- Svenska Boxerklubben (Sweden) [19]
- Boxer Review (Serbia) [20]

Bullmastiff

The **Bullmastiff** is a powerful dog, which was originally a cross between the English Mastiff and the Old English Bulldog. Originally bred to find and immobilize poachers, the breed has become popular as a family pet.

Appearance

Size

Males should be tall (AKC Std.) at the withers and . Females should be at the withers, and . Exceeding these dimensions is discouraged by breeders as a larger dog may be too cumbersome to be agile enough to properly perform the job for which the breed was created.

Color

Bullmastiffs are described as fawn, red, or brindle. These are the only acceptable colors in the AKC standard. The fawn can range from a very light brown to a reddish brown. Red can range from a light red-fawn to a dark rich red. Brindles are a striped overlay of the fawn or red. A Bullmastiff should have no white markings, except for on the chest where a little white is allowed. See breed standard under external links for additional details

Temperament

A Bullmastiff should be confident, yet docile. A Bullmastiff is courageous, extremely loyal to its family, calm, and loving. Bullmastiffs become intensely attached to their families.

Bullmastiffs can also get along with other dogs, but it is common for males not to get along with other males. The Bullmastiff can get along extremely well with children provided the dog has been properly trained and socialized. Parental supervision must be maintained when they are with children; as with most large dogs, they may knock smaller children down accidentally.

A Bullmastiff, because of its history, is a very independent dog, and likes to make its own decisions. However, with good training, a Bullmastiff will look to its owner for "permission" to act on its instincts. Early socialization and obedience training with all members of the family will teach the dog to look to them before taking action. They are very athletic and muscular, making them incredibly fast and agile.

They were never bred for hunting purposes, and rarely show signs of aggression. The Bullmastiff is a sweet-natured breed.

Health

The lifespan for a Bullmastiff is generally from eight to ten years. A Bullmastiff will not stop growing until it is about two and one half years of age. Bullmastiffs are prone to certain hereditary diseases including:

- Hip dysplasia, affecting 24.5% of specimens
- Elbow dysplasia, affecting 13.8% of specimens
- Entropion
- Hypothyroidism affecting 2.8% of specimens
- Lymphoma cancer
- Progressive retinal atrophy, a particular problem since the trait is an autosomal dominant one.
- Arthritis
- Bloat

Cosmetic genetic problems include longhairs and Dudley's. These are recessives and not common. The Dudley, named after a notable Bulldog breeder of the 1800s, the Earl of Dudley, is a lack of pigment in the mask. It can be liver colored or simply not present. These dogs can be confused with Dogue de Bordeauxs even if you know the breeds well.

History

Bred by English gamekeepers in the 1800s to assist English wardens or gamekeepers guard estates. As a result the Bullmastiff is known as the Gamekeeper's Night Dog. The Bullmastiff was a cross of 40% Old English Bulldog (not the short, chubby Bulldog of today) and 60% English Mastiff for its size, strength and loyalty. They bark much less often than other breeds, however, they will bark on alarm.

The Bullmastiff was recognized as a pure-bred dog in 1924 by the English Kennel Club.

In October, 1933, The American Kennel Club recognized the Bullmastiff. The first standard for the breed was approved in 1935.

The standard has undergone several revisions since then. The most current version is available on the AKC web site.

Bullmastiffs in popular culture

- Miikka Kiprusoff has a Bullmastiff named Reiska.
- Robbie Williams has a Bullmastiff named Duke.
- Franklin D. Roosevelt owned a Bullmastiff named Blaze.
- Agent 11 Spot from See Spot Run was a Bullmastiff.
- Butkus from the movie Rocky was actually one of Sylvester Stallone's own Bullmastiffs.
- Paul Sr., the owner of Orange County Choppers, has two Bullmastiffs named Gus and Marty.
- The video for the John Conlee song Doghouse used a Bullmastiff named Sachmo.
- Reverend Frank (Robin Williams) owns a Bullmastiff in License to Wed.
- In the movie "The Hound of the Baskervilles" (1939) the hound was a Bullmastiff chosen for his abnormally large size for that of a dog, and of the breed in particular.
- In the movie Fancy Pants (1950) the dog chase scene near the end of the film includes a Bullmastiff.
- Singer Christina Aguilera has a Bullmastiff named Cocoa. [3]
- In the movie "Dickie Roberts: Former Child Star", the family dog was a Bullmastiff.
- The comic strip Pooch Café has a Bullmastiff named Droolia as a regular character. [4]
- In the movie "Frank", the main character is a Bullmastiff. [5]
- The 1999 movie, The Dogwalker is about a woman who owned a Bullmastiff.
- Cujo - a playful ghost dog from Danny Phantom turns into a 30 ft overgrown Bullmastiff when angered.
- "Hotel for Dogs" has a Bullmastiff as a major character.
- "Hooch" in the Tom Hanks movie "Turner and Hooch" is often mistaken for a Bullmastiff. Hooch is actually a Dogue de Bordeaux (French Mastiff).
- Colin Graham, Executive Recruiter at Korn/Ferry International has a Bullmastiff named Georgia
- In the comic We3 by Grant Morrison a cyborg Bullmastiff is one the main antagonists.

- The Roloff family on Little People, Big World has a Bullmastiff named Rocky.
- The Bullmastiff is mentioned by Peter Kay when he is talking about boys who run around at weddings as he says "Just calm down will you, you're sweating like a Bullmastiff."
- Arizona Diamondbacks infielder Mark Reynolds has a Bullmastiff that he describes as "Awesome," Reynolds says. "If he hears a noise, he'll bark, then he'll run and hide. He's a big baby, and we treat him like one. I miss him when I'm on the road."
- Robert Jackstadt, Mayor of Glen Carbon, Illinois, has a Bullmastiff named Brewski.
- R&B singer Alicia Keys has a Bullmastiff named Smokey. [7]
- In Transformers: Revenge of the Fallen, Megan Fox's character Mikaela owned a Bullmastiff. Note: The dog was actually owned by Michael Bay, the producer of the film
- Jazz musician Marcus Miller has a Bullmastiff named Serena.

See also

- Mastiff

References

4. http:/ / news. yahoo. com/ s/ nm/ 20100203/ od_nm/ us_slovenia_dogs_odd;_ylt=Ammx3xqUqQG8ez. fVh7Xg3Ks0NUE;_ylu=X3oDMTFmZDI0NzkyBHBvcwMyMDUEc2VjA2FjY29yZGlvbl9vZGRfbmV3cwRzbGsDc

External links

- American Bullmastiff Association website [1]
- Bullmastiff Breed Standard (US) [2]
- Breed Standard (Canada) [3]
- Breed Standard (Great Britain) [4]

Doberman Pinscher

The **Doberman Pinscher** (alternatively spelled **Dobermann** in many countries) or simply **Doberman** is a breed of domestic dog originally developed around 1890 by Karl Friedrich Louis Dobermann. Dobermann Pinschers are among the most common of pet breeds, and the breed is well known as an intelligent, alert, and loyal companion dog. Although once commonly used as guard dogs or police dogs, this is less common today. In many countries, Dobermann Pinschers are one of the most recognizable breeds, in part because of their actual roles in society, and in part because of media attention (see temperament). Careful breeding has improved the disposition of this breed, and the modern Dobermann Pinscher is an energetic and lively breed suitable for companionship and family life.

Characteristics

Appearance

Kennel club standards describe Doberman Pinschers as dogs of medium size, square build and short coat. They are compactly built and athletic with endurance and speed. The Doberman Pinscher should have a proud, watchful, determined, and obedient temperament. The dog was originally intended as a guard dog, so males should have a masculine, muscular, noble appearance. Females are thinner, but should not be spindly.

Size and proportions

The Doberman Pinscher is a dog of medium size. Although the breed standards vary among kennel and breed clubs, the dog typically stands between 26 to 28 inches 27.5 being ideal (66 to 72 cm), the female is typically somewhere between 24 to 26 inches, 25.5 being ideal (61 to 68 cm). The Doberman has a square frame: its length should equal its height to the withers, and the length of its head, neck and legs should be in proportion to its body.

There are no standards for the weight of the Doberman Pinscher. The ideal dog must have sufficient size for an optimal combination of strength, endurance and agility. The male generally weighs between 75 and 100 pounds (34 and 45 kg) and the female between 60 and 90 pounds (27 and 41 kg).

Color

Two different color genes exist in the Doberman, one for *black* (B) and one for *color dilution* (D). There are nine possible combinations of these allelles (BBDD, BBDd BbDD BbDd, BBdd, Bbdd, bbDD, bbDd, bbdd), which result in four different color phenotypes: black, red, blue, and fawn (Isabella). The traditional and most common color occurs when both the color and dilution genes have at least one dominant allele (i.e., BBDD, BBDd, BbDD or BbDd), and is commonly referred to as *black* or *black and rust* (also called black and tan). The *red*, *red rust* or *brown* coloration occurs when the black gene has two recessive alleles but the dilution gene has at least one dominant allele (i.e., bbDD, bbDd). "Blue" and "fawn" are controlled by the color dilution gene. The blue Doberman has the color gene with at least one dominant allele and the dilution gene with both recessive alleles (i.e., BBdd or Bbdd). The fawn (Isabella) coloration is the least common, occurring only when both the color and dilution genes have two recessive alleles (i.e., bbdd). Thus, the blue color is a diluted black, and the fawn color is a diluted red. Highly rare cases have been reported of an "albino Doberman," a white Doberman who does actually have pigmentation and is therefore not an albino. It is named an albino because of its light coloring, but is actually simply a whiter variation.

Expression of the color dilution gene is a disorder called Color Dilution Alopecia. Although not life threatening, these dogs can develop skin problems. Since 1994 the blue and fawn colors have been banned from breeding by the Dobermann Verein in Germany and under FCI regulations Blue and Fawn are considered disqualifying faults in the international showring.

In 1976, a "white" Doberman Pinscher bitch was whelped, and was subsequently bred to her son, who was also bred to his litter sisters. This tight inbreeding continued for some time to allow the breeders to "fix" the mutation. White dobermans are a cream color with pure white markings and icy blue eyes. Although the disorder is consistent with albinism, a proper characterization of the mutation is currently unknown. The animals are known to be tyrosinase-positive albinoids, lacking melanin in oculocutaneous structures, but no known mutation has been identified. Thus, these Doberman Pinschers are not actually white, rather they suffer from a deleterious genetic disorder that is associated with increased health risks.

Tails

The Doberman Pinscher's natural tail is fairly long, but individual dogs often have a short tail as a result of docking, a procedure in which the majority of the tail is surgically removed shortly after birth.

The practice of docking has been around for centuries, and is older than the Doberman as a breed. The putative reason for docking is to ensure that the tail does not get in the way of the dog's work. Recently, docking has become a controversial topic. The American Kennel Club standard for Doberman Pinschers includes a tail docked near the 2nd vertebrae. Docking is a common practice in North America, Russia and Japan (as well as a number of other countries with Doberman populations), where it is legal. In many European countries, docking has been made illegal, and in others it is limited.

Ears

Doberman Pinschers will often have their ears cropped, as do many other breeds, a procedure that is functionally related to breed type for both the traditional guard duty and effective sound localization. Like tail docking, ear cropping is illegal in some countries, and in these Doberman Pinschers have natural ears. Doberman Pinscher ear cropping is usually done between 7 and 9 weeks of age. Cropping done after 12 weeks has a low rate of success in getting the ears to stand. Some Doberman Pinscher owners prefer not to have their pet's ears cropped because they are concerned the procedure is painful for the animal. The process involves trimming off part of the animal's ears and propping them up with posts and tape bandages, which allows the cartilage to develop into an upright position as the puppy grows. The incision scabs fall off within a week and stitches are removed a week after that. The puppy will still have the ability to lay the ears back or down. The process of posting the ears generally takes about a month, but longer show crops can take several months. Ear posting is more discomforting to the dog than the surgery itself. Posting techniques and the associated discomfort vary from one posting technique to the next.

In some countries' conformation shows, Doberman Pinschers are allowed to compete with either cropped or natural ears. In Germany a cropped or docked dog cannot be shown regardless of country of origin. Special written exception to this policy does occur when Germany is the location for international events.

Temperament

Doberman Pinschers are the target of a mistaken stereotype of ferocity and aggression. As a personal protection dog, the Doberman was originally bred for these traits: it had to be large and intimidating, fearless and willing to defend its owner, but sufficiently obedient and restrained to only do so on command. These traits served the dog well in its role as a personal defense dog, police dog or war dog, but were not ideally adapted to a companionship role. In recent decades, the Doberman Pinscher's size, short coat, and intelligence made it a desirable house dog. Although these dogs are mistaken for their aggression, they are extremely loyal. They can easily learn to 'Respect and Protect' their owners. In response, they are excellent guard dogs that protect their loved ones. They are generally sociable towards humans and can be with other dogs, ranking among the more-likely breeds to show aggressive behaviour toward strangers and other dogs but not among the most likely. They are very unlikely to show aggressive behaviour towards their owners. There is evidence that Doberman Pinschers in North America are calmer than their European counterparts because of these breeding strategies. Because of these differences in breeding strategies, different lines of Doberman Pinschers have developed different traits. Although many contemporary Doberman Pinschers in North America are gentle, loyal, loving, and intelligent dogs, some lines are bred more true to the original personality standard.

Although the stereotype is largely mistaken, the personality of the Doberman Pinscher is peculiar to the breed. There is a great deal of scientific evidence that Doberman Pinschers have a number of stable psychological traits, such as personality factors and intelligence. As early as 1965, studies have shown that there are several broad behavioral traits that significantly predict behavior and are genetically determined. Subsequently, there have been numerous scientific attempts to quantify canine personality or temperament by using statistical techniques for assessing personality traits in humans. These studies often vary by identifying different personality factors, and by ranking breeds differently along these dimensions. One such study found that Doberman Pinschers, compared to other breeds, rank high in playfulness, average in curiosity/fearlessness, low on aggressiveness and low on sociability. Another such study ranked Doberman Pinschers low on reactivity/surgence, and high on aggression/disagreeableness and openness/trainability

Intelligence

Canine intelligence is an umbrella term that encompasses the faculties involved in a wide range of mental tasks, such as learning, problem-solving and communication. The Doberman Pinscher has ranked amongst the most intelligent of dog breeds in experimental studies and expert evaluations. For instance, Psychologist Stanley Coren ranks the Doberman as the 5th most intelligent dog in the category of *obedience command training* based on the selective surveys he performed of some trainers as documented in his book The Intelligence of Dogs. Additionally, in two studies, Hart and Hart (1985) ranked the Doberman Pinscher first in this category, and Tortora (1980) gave the Doberman the highest rank in trainability, as does Howe. Although the methods of evaluation differ, these studies consistently show that the Doberman Pinscher, along with the Border Collie, German Shepherd and Standard Poodle, is one of the most trainable breeds of dog.

Aggression

In addition to the studies of canine personality, there has been some research to determine whether there are breed differences in aggression. In a recent study, aggression was divided into four categories: aggression directed at strangers, owner, other strange dogs and rivalry with other household dogs. This study found that the Doberman Pinscher ranked relatively high on stranger-directed aggression (behind the Dachshund and Chihuahua), but extremely low on owner-directed aggression. The Doberman Pinscher ranked as average on dog-directed aggression and dog rivalry. Looking only at bites and attempted bites, Doberman Pinschers rank as far less aggressive towards humans, and show less aggression than many breeds without a reputation (e.g., Cocker Spaniel, Border Collie and Great Dane). This study concluded that aggression has a genetic basis, that the Doberman shows a distinctive pattern of aggression depending on the situation, and that contemporary Doberman Pinschers are not an aggressive breed overall.

Although recent studies do not rank Doberman Pinschers as the most aggressive breed, their size, strength and aggression towards strangers makes them potentially dangerous. Studies of dog bites and dog bite fatalities have shown that the danger of attack by Dobermans is relatively high, and that children are five times as likely to be bitten by a Doberman as a Labrador Retriever. According to the Centers for Disease Control and Prevention, between 1979 and 1998, the Doberman Pinscher was involved in attacks on humans resulting in fatalities less frequently than several other dog breeds such as pit bull–type dogs, German Shepherd Dogs, Rottweilers, ·Husky-type, Wolf-dog hybrids and Alaskan Malamutes. According to this Center for Disease Control and Prevention study, one of the most important factors contributing to dog bites are related to the level of responsibility exercised by dog owners.

Health

On average, Doberman Pinschers live about 10–14 years, and they frequently suffer from a number of health concerns. Common serious health problems include dilated cardiomyopathy, cervical vertebral instability (CVI), von Willebrand's disease (a bleeding disorder for which genetic testing of has been available since 2000 - the test enables both parents of a prospective litter to be tested for the carrier gene, thus preventing inheritance of the disease), and prostatic disease. Less serious common health concerns include hypothyroidism and hip dysplasia.

Studies have shown that the Doberman Pinscher suffers from prostatic diseases, (such as bacterial prostatiti, prostatic cysts, prostatic adenocarcinoma, and benign hyperplasia) more than any other breed. Neutering can significantly reduce these risks (see Dog for information).

Dilated cardiomyopathy is a major cause of death in Doberman Pinschers. This disease affects Dobermans more than any other breed. Nearly 40% of DCM diagnoses are for Doberman Pinschers, followed by German Shepherds at 13%. Research has shown that the breed is affected by an *attenuated wavy fiber* type of DCM that affects many other breeds, as well as an additional, *fatty infiltration-degenerative* type that appears to be specific to Doberman Pinscher and Boxer breeds. This serious disease is likely to be fatal in most Doberman Pinschers affected Across multiple studies, more than half of the Doberman Pinschers studied develop the condition. Roughly a quarter of Doberman Pinschers who developed cardiomyopathy died suddenly from unknown causes, and an additional fifty percent died of congestive heart failure In addition to being more prevalent, this disease is also more serious in Doberman Pinschers. Following diagnosis, the average non-Doberman has an expected survival time of 8 months; for Doberman Pinschers, the expected survival time is less than 2 months. Although the causes for the disease are largely unknown, there is evidence that it is a familial disease inherited as an autosomal dominant trait. Investigation into the genetic causes of canine DCM may lead to therapeutic and breeding practices to limit its impact

History

Doberman Pinschers were first bred in the town of Apolda, in the German state of Thuringia around 1890, following the Franco-Prussian War by Karl Friedrich Louis Dobermann. Dobermann served in the dangerous role of local tax collector, and ran the Apolda dog pound. With access to dogs of many breeds, he aimed to create a breed that would be ideal for protecting him during his collections, which took him through many bandit-infested areas. He set out to breed a new type of dog that, in his opinion, would be the perfect combination of strength, loyalty, intelligence, and ferocity. Later, Otto Goeller and Philip Gruening continued to develop the breed to become the dog that is seen today.

The breed is believed to have been created from several different breeds of dogs that had the characteristics that Dobermann was looking for, including the German Pinscher, the Beauceron, the Rottweiler, the Thuringian Sylvan Dog, the Greyhound, the Great Dane, the Weimaraner, the German Shorthaired Pointer, the Manchester Terrier and the Old German Shepherd Dog. The exact ratios of mixing, and even the exact breeds that were used, remain uncertain to this day, although many experts believe that the Doberman Pinscher is a combination of at least four of these breeds. The single exception is the documented crossing with the Greyhound and Manchester Terrier. It is also widely believed that the old German Shepherd gene pool was the single largest contributor to the Doberman breed. A book entitled *The Dobermann Pinscher*, written by Philip Greunig (first printing in 1939), is considered the foremost study of the development of the breed by one of its most ardent students. It describes the breed's early development by Otto Goeller, whose hand allowed the Doberman to become the dog we recognize today.

After Dobermann's death in 1894, the Germans named the breed Dobermann-pinscher in his honor, but a half century later dropped the pinscher on the grounds that this German word for terrier was no longer appropriate. The British did the same a few years later.

Famous Doberman Pinschers

- Ch. Rancho Dobe's Storm: back to back Westminster Best in Show (1952, 1953). [1]
- Bingo von Ellendonk: first Dobermann to score 300 points (perfect score) in Schutzhund. [2]
- Ch. Cambria Cactus Cash: Sired 144 AKC champions as of June 2007.[3]
- Graf Belling v. Grönland: first registered Dobermann. [4]

Fictional Doberman Pinschers

- Sniper from *Ginga: Nagareboshi Gin*
- Alpha from the movie *Up*
- Luca from *Garfield: The Movie*
- Roscoe and DeSoto from *Oliver and Company*
- 1991 film Eyes Of An Angel starring John Travolta has its plot around a dobermann.

Dogue de Bordeaux

The **Dogue de Bordeaux**, **Bordeaux Mastiff** or **French Mastiff** or **Bordeauxdog** is a breed of dog that is strong, powerful, and imposing. The Dogue de Bordeaux is one of the most ancient French breeds. They are a typical brachycephalic molossoid type. Bordeaux are very powerful dogs, with a very muscular body yet retaining a harmonious temperament. The breed has been utilized in many different forms, from using their brawn to pull carts or haul heavy objects, to guarding flocks and used to protect castles of the European elite.

Description

Appearance

Dogue de Bordeaux, also called French Mastiff or Bordeaux Bulldog, lower to the ground than is long, well muscled and stocky Molosser breed with a heavy, broad head.

Weight

The breed standards by European FCI and American Kennel Club specify minimum weight of 99 lbs for a female and 110 lbs for a male. There is no formally stated maximum weight but dogs must be balanced with regard to their overall type and the conformation standards of the breed.

Height

The standard states that the desirable height, at maturity, should range between 23½ inches to 27 inches (58-67.5 cm) for male dogs and from 22½ inches to 25½ inches (57 cm-65 cm) for females. Deviation from these margins is considered a fault.

General conformation

Dogue de Bordeaux is a well balanced, muscular and massive dog with a powerful build. The Dogue's size should come mostly from width and muscles, rather than height. The breed is set somewhat low to the ground and not tall like the English Mastiff. The body of the Dogue de Bordeaux is thick-set, with a short, straight top-line and a gentle rounded croup. The front legs should be straight and heavy-boned. The straight tail begins thickly at the base and then tapers to a point at the end. It should not reach lower than the hocks. The tail is thick at the base and tapers to the tip and is set and carried low. The breed is to be presented in a completely natural condition with intact ears, tail and natural dewclaws. It should be evaluated equally for correctness in conformation, temperament, movement and overall structural soundness.

Head

The massive head is a crucial breed characteristic. The Dogue de Bordeaux is claimed to have the largest head in the canine world, in proportion to the rest of the body. For males the circumference of the head, measured at the widest point of the skull, is roughly equal to the dog's height at the withers (shoulders). For females the circumference may be slightly less. When viewed from the front or from above, the head of the Dogue forms a trapezoid shape with the longer top-line of the skull, and the shorter line of the underjaw, forming the parallel sides of the trapezoid. The jaw is undershot and powerful. The Dogue should always have a black or red mask that can be distinguished from the rest of the coat around and under the nose, including the lips and eye rims. The muzzle should be at most 1/3 the total length of the head and no shorter than 1/4 the length of the head, the ideal being between the two extremes. The upper lips hang thickly down over the lower jaw. The skin on the neck is loose, forming a noticeable dewlap, but should not be excessive like that of a Neapolitan Mastiff. Small pendant ears top the head, but should not be long and houndy.

Coat

The standard specifies the coat to be 'short, fine, and soft to the touch'. Color varies from shades of fawn (light, coppery red) to mahogany (dark, brownish red)or also a orange skin with a black, brown or red mask, though the red mask is true to the breed. White markings are permitted on the tips of the toes and on the chest, but white on any other part of the body is considered a fault, and a disqualifying one if the pigmentation goes beyond the neck.

Litter size

As with any breed, litter sizes may vary from dog to dog. An average dog has five to eight puppies, although the Dogue de Bordeaux usually has between ten to sixteen pups.

Temperament

The Dogue de Bordeaux is even-tempered, protective by nature, and is vigilant but without aggressiveness. Dogues de Bordeaux are extremely attached and devoted to their family. They are calm and balanced with high stimulus thresholds. The Dogue is intelligent and can also be stubborn, arrogant, and dominant. Early socialization for this breed is an absolute must.

History

The Dogue de Bordeaux was known in France as early as the fourteenth century particularly in southern France in the region around Bordeaux. Hence, the city lent its name to these large dogs.

A uniform breed type of the Bordeaux Dog did not exist before about 1920. The French placed emphasis on keeping the old breeding line pure. Black masks were considered an indication of the crossing in of the English Mastiff. As an important indication of purity of the breed, attention was paid to the self colored (pink) nose, lighter eye color (dark amber), and red mask. They were originally bred with huge anatomically incorrect heads; a pioneer for the breed in Germany, Werner Preugschat once wrote:

"What am I supposed to do with a dog that has a monstrous skull and is at most able to carry it from the food dish to its bed?"

The Dogue de Bordeaux was at one time, known to come in two varieties, Dogues and Doguins, the former, the Dogue, being a considerably larger dog than the latter. The latter, the Doguin, has withered away to nothing more than a mention in breed history books, as it is no longer in existence.

The history of the breed is believed to predate the Bullmastiff and the Bulldog. It is said that the Dogue can be found in the background of the Bullmastiff, and others claim that the Dogue and Mastiff breeds were both being accomplished at the same time. Another theory is the Dogue de Bordeaux originates from the Tibetan Mastiff and it is also said that the Dogue is related to the Greco Roman molossoids used for war, as there was a breed similar to the Dogue de Bordeaux in Rome at the time of Julius Caesar's reign, possibly a cousin of the Neapolitan Mastiff. Others suggest that the Dogue de Bordeaux is a descendent of a breed which existed in ancient France, the Dogues de Bordeaux of Aquitaine. Which ever theory is true, it is obvious that the Dogue de Bordeaux shares the same common links as all modern molossers.

The Dogue de Bordeaux was once classified into three varieties, the Parisian, the Toulouse and the Bordeaux, types which were bred depending on the region of France and the jobs they were required to do. Ancestral Dogues de Bordeaux had various coat colors, such as brindle and majority of white markings that carried fully up the legs. They had scissor bites in some regions, undershot in others, big heads, small heads, large bodies and small bodies, very inconsistent in type. Another controversial aspect was the mask, red (brown), none or black. The Dogues de Bordeaux of Bordeaux of the time also sported cropped ears. Regardless, they all had a general type similar to today's Dogue de Bordeaux.

In 1863 the first canine exhibition was held at the "Jardin d'Acclimatation" in Paris, France. The winner of the Dogue de Bordeaux was a bitch named Magentas. The Dogue de Bordeaux was then given the name of the capital of their region of origin, today's Dogue de Bordeaux.

The Dogue de Bordeaux was used as a hunter, a herding dog, and a guardian. They were trained to bait bulls, bears, and jaguars, hunt boars, herd cattle, and protect the homes, butcher shops, and vineyards of their masters. The Dogue de Bordeaux was prized as protectors and was often found in the homes of the wealthy of France. A setback in the breed came during the French Revolution when many of the Dogues de Bordeaux perished with their wealthy masters. The Dogues de Bordeaux of the common man have thrived. These became champions, and were powerful dogs bred to do their jobs and do them well. Another setback for the breed was during World War II, Adolf Hitler was said to have demanded the execution of all Dogues de Bordeaux because of their devout loyalty to their owners.

During the 1960s, a group of breeders of the Dogue de Bordeaux in France, headed by Raymond Triquet, worked on the rebuilding of the foundation of the breed. In 1970 a new standard was written for the breed, with the most recent update in 1995. This standard is the basis of the standard written for the AKC in 2005.

Although the Dogue de Bordeaux first came to the USA in the 1890s for the show ring, the first documented Dogues de Bordeaux of modern times was in 1959, Fidelle de Fenelon, and in 1968, Rugby de la Maison des Arbres. Between 1969 and 1980 imported Dogues de Bordeaux in the USA were scarce, limited to a few breeders who worked closely with the French Dogue de Bordeaux Club, the SADB. The breed was first "officially" introduced to American purebred enthusiasts in an article written in 1982 and by the American anthropologist, Dr. Carl Semencic for "Dog World" magazine. That article, entitled "Introducing the Dogue de Bordeaux", was followed by chapters dedicated to the Dogue in Semencic's books on dogs, published by T.F.H. Publications of Neptune, New Jersey. When Semencic's first article on the breed was published there were no Bordeaux Dogues in the United States, there were 600 examples left in the world, mostly in France, Holland and East Berlin, and the breed's numbers were on the decline. Much later, in 1989 the typical American family saw the Dogue de Bordeaux for the first time on the big screen in Touchstone's movie *Turner & Hooch* about a police man and his canine partner, although many people did not know that the massive slobbering animal was a Dogue de Bordeaux.

Since then the Dogue de Bordeaux has taken hold in the United States and can be found in greatly increasing numbers across the country. The Dogue de Bordeaux has been supported by multiple breed clubs throughout the years, and has finally found its way to full AKC recognition through the assistance of the Dogue de Bordeaux Society of America. Since 1997 the DDBSA has helped bring the breed to the point in which full AKC recognition could be achieved.

The Dogue de Bordeaux has begun to flourish is recent years, with the introduction of them into more movies and even television, as well as their full recognition status by the American Kennel Club, also known as the AKC (full AKC recognition began July 2008). Their numbers are climbing, but careful attention must be paid to health in the breed, if the increase in popularity is to progress this breed in a positive forward motion in years to come.

- Beasley, who played the title role of Hooch in *Turner & Hooch.*
- Foster, who was the Spencer family dog on *General Hospital.*
- Mac, owned by Dutch footballer Andy van der Meyde, famously stolen and found in 2006.

- Kalusha De El Siscar, a female, appeared with Sarah Jessica Parker in *Sex and the City*.
- England Football player Frank Lampard owns several Dogues de Bordeaux and has offered several puppies of the same breed to Chelsea FC fans.
- English TV presenter Paul Ross has a Dogue de Bordeaux which appeared in Your dog magazine.
- Edward Norton's character in *The Italian Job* had Dogues guarding his estate.
- Maria Bello's character in the movie *Payback* had a Dogue de Bordeaux, named Porter.
- NHL superstar Evgeni Malkin also has a Dogue de Bordeaux, one his parents are currently attempting to move from Russia to Pittsburgh, PA.
- England national football team player Wayne Rooney has also revealed that he owns one of these dogs

Further reading

Janish, Joseph. *Dogue de Bordeaux* Kennel Club Books, 2003. ISBN 1-59378-215-2

"The Saga of the Dogue de Bordeaux" written by Raymond Triquet and published by Bas Bosch Press

"The World of Dogues De Bordeaux". Published by Bas Bosch Press

See also

- Argentine Dogo

External links

- The Dogue de Bordeaux Society of America [1]
- The Dogue de Bordeaux Rescue of America [2]
- North American Bordeaux Federation [3]
- Canadian Dogue de Bordeaux Club [4]
- Bordeaux Club of Great Britain [5]
- La Société des Amateurs de Dogues de Bordeaux [6], in the French language.
- American Kennel Club [7]
- http://stellardoguedebordeaux.com/Stellar Dogue de Bordeaux

German Pinscher

The **German Pinscher** (original name Deutscher Pinscher, FCI No. 184) is a medium-sized, breed of dog, a Pinscher type that originated in Germany. The breed is included in the origins of the Dobermann, the Miniature Pinscher, the Affenpinscher, Miniature Schnauzer, Giant Schnauzer and the Standard Schnauzer. The breed is rising in numbers in the U.S., mainly due to their full acceptance to AKC in 2003. In Australia the breed is established with a rise in popularity becoming evident. There are Australian bred dogs in many breeding kennels worldwide including the USA, Finland, Sweden and Spain.

Appearance

The German Pinscher is a moderately small sized dog, usually weighing between 25-35 pounds and typically 17-20 inches in height, with a short coat. The ideal German Pinscher is elegant in appearance with a strong square build and moderate body structure, muscular and powerful for endurance and agility.

Colors for this breed include black and tan, blue, red, fawn, and tan. For all countries where the Fédération Cynologique Internationale standard applies, only black and tan and solid red are allowed colors.

There are also a few colors for this breed that became extinct during the world wars of the twentieth century. These include solid black and salt-and-pepper as well as harlequin.

The coat should be short and dense, smooth and close lying.

History

The Wire Haired and Smooth Haired Pinschers, as the Standard Schnauzer and German Pinscher were originally called, were shown in dog books as early as 1884. However drawings of the Germans Pinscher date back to at least 1780, and the breed likely traces its roots to varieties of ratters well established on farms in Germany as far back as the 15th century. These medium-sized dogs descended from early European herding and guardian breeds.

The source of the German Pinscher can be followed back until 1836 when this breed surpassed the Mops in popularity. Pinschers were used as guard dogs for coaches. They also lived in homesteads where they were used to kill rats, a job they did instinctually and independently. This behavior did not need to be trained into the German Pinscher; even today you can observe German Pinschers searching for and finding rats in open areas and in homesteads. This high prey drive is a good reason not to leave a German Pinscher off lead outside of a fenced area.

The Standard Schnauzer (then referred to as the Wire Haired Pinscher) was originally born in the same litter as the German Pincher. Over time, breeders decided to separate the "varieties," changing them to actual "breeds". After three generations of the same coat were born, the Pinscher-Schnauzer club allowed them to be registered as their respective "breed".

From 1950 to 1958 no litter had been registered. Credit is attributed to Werner Jung for collecting several of the breed in 1958 to continue the line.

The German Pinscher came to breeders in the United States in the early 1980s, though accounts of singular German Pinschers appearing in the country before then have been noted. In 1985, the German Pinscher Club of America was started by various German Pinscher fanciers, most of whom are no longer active in the breed. At this time, the German Pinscher was shown in rare breed shows. They were also recognized by the United Kennel Club.

The German Pinscher gained full acceptance by the Canadian Kennel Club[1] in 2000. The CKC named Ch Othello des Charmettes its first Champion on April 20, 2000. The German Pinscher gained full acceptance by the American Kennel Club [2] in 2003. The AKC named Ch Riward's Rollin Rocs Rusty (Jambo de la Capelliere[3] x Windamir's Zarra) its first Champion on January 8, 2003.

In 2004, the German Pinscher competed at its first Westminster Kennel Club[4] show. The Best of Breed winner was Ch. Windamir Hunter des Charmettes [5](Windamir's Sayzar x Lot T Da Des Charmettes). The Best of Opposite Sex to Best of Breed was Ch. Windamir's Chosen One [6] (Tanner's Morning Star x Windmir's A-blazin at RG's).

Extinct varieties

There are several now-extinct varieties of the German Pinscher. Among them are:

- Harlekinpinscher (Harlequin Pinscher, for the merle coloration)
- Schweizer Pinscher (also called the Jonataler Pinscher, Pfisterlinge, Silberpinsch, Swiss Salt and Pepper Pinscher, Swiss Shorthair Pinscher)
- Seidenpinscher (also called the German Silky Pinscher, Silky Pinscher)

Some of these may have recently been re-formed from the German Pinscher and marketed as rare breeds for those seeking unique pets.

Health and temperament

Temperament

A well bred German Pinscher will be a loving companion with an even temperament. Temperament is hereditary. When considering adding a German Pinscher to a family, it is advised to be able to meet and touch the mother of the puppy you are offered. German Pinschers are generally friendly dogs. They are highly intelligent, quick learners who do not enjoy repetition in training. A well bred German Pinscher can be trusted with small animals and children, though no dog should ever be left unsupervised with either. If the puppy shies away when faced with strangers, it may be a sign of poor breeding.

It should also be noted that German Pinschers are very high energy dogs, in many cases requiring *several hours* of exercise a day. Accordingly, a large, securely fenced, yard (or some other means of providing the dog with the necessary physical and mental exercise on a *daily* basis) is highly recommended for anyone considering the breed as a pet.

Health

Due to the small gene pool of the German Pinscher, breeders should health test their dogs for hereditary cataracts, hip and elbow displaysia, von Willebrand disease, thyroid disorder and with the increased incidences of Cardiac Disease due to irresponsible breeding practices, German Pinschers suspect for heart issues should be removed from all breeding programs.

External links

- Breed clubs
    - The German Pinscher Club of America [7]
    - The German Pinscher Club UK [8]
    - The German Pinscher Club of Victoria [9]
- Information
    - GermanPinschers.com - Description of the Breed [10]
    - American Kennel Club - German Pinscher [11]
    - Westminster Kennel Club - German Pinscher [12]
    - Dog Breed Info Center - German Pinscher [13]
- Rescue
    - German Pinscher Rescue [14]

Giant Schnauzer

The **Giant Schnauzer** is a large, powerful, and compact breed of dog. It is one of the three Schnauzer breeds. Like most large breeds, the Giant Schnauzer needs a fair amount of exercise.

Appearance

When hand-stripped, the Giant Schnauzer has a harsh, wiry outer coat and dense, soft undercoat. Coat color is either black or salt and pepper (grey). It weighs between 70 and 100 lb (32 to 45 kg) and stands 23.5 to 27.5 in (59 to 70 cm) at the withers.

When moving at a fast trot, a properly built Giant Schnauzer will single-track. Back remains strong, firm, and flat.

The American Kennel Club lists the Giant as low shedding - and therefore hypoallergenic - along with both other breeds of Schnauzers. However, Giant Schnauzers, as with almost all dogs, do shed. When allowed, the hair on a Schnauzer will grow long, which increases shedding, and thereby potentially increasing allergens. This can be mitigated with consistent grooming to include mostly Long hair. The Giant Schnauzer does not moult.

Temperament

The Giant Schnauzer is a great dog if one is looking for a playful yet guarding protector. For those who like the large dogs, the size of the Giant can be very discouraging for any would-be offender, but it is not necessarily a Gentle Giant as say the Great Dane. Some tend to have a herding instinct at a young age so it is best to teach puppies or younger dogs to not nip or mouth at all. In many cases it has led to the dog going straight back to the breeder or worse, a shelter. Some Giants can be dog aggressive, but that is common with all Schnauzers. Poorly socialized dogs will have themselves a problem of a large dog unwelcoming of house guests and showing aggression towards other dogs. Some have even shown aggression to just female sexes.

This is a working breed and such requires some amount of exercise or troubling behaviors may occur to relinquish that bored state they may have. A good jog or a let loose in a park with other dogs and maybe a water source will give the owner a well-mannered and tired friend coming home. They are a water breed, which means unless the owner wants to give a bath after their dog has been soaking in a well filled ditch or pond, proper training will be needed or Giants will jump head first into any body of water to swim and even drink. They are not a breed that will take off the moment one lets them off the leash. Some will even turn back mid-stride to make sure their owner is near and may even turn back if too far away. This is not to say to let a dog off in an open park as there are of course risks, especially with leash laws, but they are a distinguishing breed than most that would take off and not look back. Using caution will minimize the risk.

The Giant has received four stars out of five on protection. They will let their owner know a car or even footsteps approaching the house far before a human would identify. They have a sort of howling bark that makes them sound larger than life to said-offenders and that in itself will probably do the trick. If not, one will have a dog that upon the slightest hint of an attack will launch itself in soaring fashion at the offender. Due to their terrier heritage they will shake whatever part of the body they latch onto which no doubt will cause the intruder who was looking for an easy will pick to leave limping. However, such a protective nature may lead to people aggression if not properly socialized. This is not a dog to stick in the backyard and leave it at that. Acquaintances, friends and even family members can find themselves on the wrong end of the Giant's massive mouth which will lead to much bigger legal problems if blood is drawn. Proper training and socialization will have this particular breed at one's side as a well-mannered companion.

The Giant Schnauzer is a powerful breed that demands a steady, yet very gentle hand and with proper leadership, this large breed can not only be a couch companion and jogging partner, but a loyal and a not too overprotective friend that will take a bullet for its owner.

Health problems

Health problems in the breed include:

- Autoimmune diseases (hypothyroidism, Autoimmune hemolytic anemia (AIHA) (also called Immune Mediated Hemolytic Anemia (IMHA)), SLO, Crohn's disease, and so on)
- Epilepsy
- Hip dysplasia
- Incontinence
- Toe Cancer

History

Giants have been described as far back as 1832 from cattle and pig farms in the Bavarian highlands region of Germany and has been called oblanders, although a written breed standard was not established until 1923. It was at this time (breed description and showing of these dogs) that some breeders used standard schnauzers to help fix the schnauzer type and developed the central German type Giant Schnauzer. The Munich type and oblanders were used for power and size.

After World War I, the Giant Schnauzer was significantly reduced in numbers. The Kennel (Kinzigtal) owned by C. Clalaminus, contributed to reestablishing the breed. It was this kennel that admitted to three crosses to dogs of other breeds to assist with dominant black colour, well-crested neck and correct head proportions. It is speculated that the black Great Dane, and or the Bouvier des Roulers may have been the breed of the three unknown crosses. Still the foundation stock was oblanders to which oversize standard schnauzers were added.

See also

- Standard Schnauzer
- Miniature Schnauzer

References

- Fogle, Bruce, DVM (2000). *The new Encyclopedia of the Dog*. Doring Kindersley (DK). ISBN 0-7894-6130-7.
- Mehus-Roe, Kristin (ed.) (2005). *The original dog bible : the definitive source for all things dog*. BowTie Press. ISBN 1-931993-34-3.
- Gallant, Johan (1996). "The world or Schnauzers: Standard - Giant - Miniature". Alpine publications. ISBN 0-931866-93-6

External links

- Breed clubs
  - Giant Schnauzer Club of America [1]
  - Giant Schnauzer Canada [2]
  - Working Riesenschnauzer Federation [3]
  - Giant Schnauzer Club [4]
- Information
  - American Kennel Club - Giant Schnauzer [5]
  - G.I.A.N.T. Schnauzer Rescue Network [6]
  - SLO autoimmune disease description [7]
  - AIHA disease description [8]
- Giant Schnauzers in the Media
  - Greatest American Dog - Kenji [9]
  - Giants Saves Owners life from burning home [10]
- Forum [11]

Great Dane

The **Great Dane** (18th Cent. French: *Grand Danois*), also known as **German Mastiff** () or **Danish Hound** (), is a breed of domestic dog (*Canis lupus familiaris*) known for its giant size. The breed is commonly referred to as the "Apollo of all breeds". The Great Dane is one of the world's tallest dog breeds. The current world record holder, measuring from paw to shoulder; from head to tail, is George. The previous Great Dane to hold the world record as tallest living dog was Gibson, who was tall at the withers and on his hind legs.

Description

Appearance

As described by the American Kennel Club, "The Great Dane combines, in its regal appearance, dignity, strength and elegance with grand size and a well-formed body. One of the largest working breeds, it never appears ugly."

The Great Dane is a short haired breed with a strong galloping figure. In the ratio between length and height, the Great Dane should be square. The male dog should not be less than at the shoulders, a female . Danes under minimum height are disqualified.

From year to year, the tallest living dog is typically a Great Dane. Previous record holders include Gibson and Titan, however the currently record holder is a blue Great Dane named Giant George who stands at the shoulder. He is also the tallest dog on record (according Guinness World Records), beating the previous holder who was a brindle Great Dane named Shamgret Danzas, who stood at the shoulder.

The minimum weight for a Great Dane over eighteen months is for males, for females. Unusually, the American Kennel Club dropped the minimum weight requirement from its standard. The male should appear more massive throughout than the female, with a larger frame and heavier bone.

Great Danes have naturally floppy, triangular ears. In the past, when Great Danes were commonly used to hunt boars, cropping of the ears was performed to make injuries to the dogs' ears less likely during hunts. Now that Danes are primarily companion animals, cropping is sometimes still done for traditional and cosmetic reasons. Today, the practice is somewhat common in the United States and much less common in Europe. In some European countries such as the United Kingdom, Ireland, Denmark, Germany, parts of Australia, and in New Zealand, the practice is banned, or controlled to only be performed by veterinary surgeons.

Coat colors

There are six show-acceptable coat colors for Great Danes:

- **Fawn**: The color is yellow gold with a black mask. Black should appear on the eye rims and eyebrows, and may appear on the ears.
- **Brindle**: The color is fawn and black in a chevron stripe pattern. Often also they are referred to as having a tiger-stripe pattern.
- **Blue**: The color is a pure steel blue. White markings at the chest and toes are not desirable and considered faults.
- **Black**: The color is a glossy black. White markings at the chest and toes are not desirable and considered faults.
- **Harlequin**: The base color is pure white with black torn patches irregularly and well distributed over the entire body; a pure white neck is preferred. The black patches should never be large enough to give the appearance of a blanket, nor so small as to give a stippled or dappled effect. Eligible, but less desirable, are a few small grey patches (this grey is consistent with a Merle marking) or a white base with single black hairs showing through, which tend to give a salt and pepper or dirty effect. (Have the same link to deafness and blindness as Merle and white danes.)
- **Mantle** (in some countries referred to as Bostons due to the similar coloration and pattern as a Boston Terrier): The color is black and white with a solid black blanket extending over the body; black skull with white muzzle; white blaze is optional; whole white collar preferred; a white chest; white on part or whole of forelegs and hind legs; white tipped black tail. A small white marking in the black blanket is acceptable, as is a break in the white collar.

Other colors occur occasionally but are not acceptable for conformation showing, and they are not pursued by breeders who intend to breed show dogs. These colors include white, fawnequin, merle, merlequin, fawn mantle, and others. Some breeders may attempt to charge more for puppies of these "rare" colors. However, the breeding of white and merle Danes is particularly controversial, as these colors may be associated with genes that produce deafness. Although they cannot be shown, white or merle Danes can usually still be registered as pedigree dogs.

Temperament

The Great Dane's large and imposing appearance belies its friendly nature; the breed is often referred to as a gentle giant. Great Danes are generally well-disposed toward other dogs, other non-canine pets and humans, although, when feeling threatened, have been known to attack humans. This is usually brought on by an unfamiliar person to the dog . Some breeds may chase or attack small animals, but this is not typical with Great Danes.

Exercise

Like most dogs, Great Danes require daily walks to remain healthy. However it is important not to over exercise this breed, particularly when young. Great Dane puppies grow very large, very fast, which puts them at risk of joint and bone problems. Because of a puppy's natural energy, Dane owners often take steps to minimize activity while the dog is still growing.

Health

Great Danes, like most giant dogs, have a fairly slow metabolism. This results in less energy and less food consumption per pound of dog than in small breeds. Great Danes have some health problems that are common to large breeds, including gastric dilatation-volvulus (GDV) (a painful distending and twisting of the stomach). This is a critical condition that can affect Great Danes and other deep-chested breeds, and which may cause death if not quickly addressed. Drinking large amounts of fluid in a short period of time can provoke GDV in Great Danes, as well as other larger breeds of dogs. It is a commonly recommended practice for Great Danes to have their stomachs tacked (Gastropexy) to the right abdominal wall if the dog or its relatives have a history of GDV, though some veterinary surgeons will not do the operation if the actual sickness has not occurred. Elevated food dishes are often believed to help prevent GDV by regulating the amount of air that is inhaled while eating, although one study suggests that they may increase the risk. Refraining from exercise or activity immediately before and after meals may also reduce risk, although this has not been validated with research. Signs that GDV may have occurred include, but are not limited to, visible distension (enlargement of the abdomen) and repeated retching that resembles repetitive non-productive attempts to vomit. GDV is a condition that is distinct from another condition referred to as bloat; though, bloat may precede the development of GDV. GDV is a surgical emergency; immediate veterinary evaluation should be sought if a dog demonstrates signs of this condition.

Breed clubs health surveys in the UK and US put the average life span of Great Danes at 6.5 to 7 years.

Dilated cardiomyopathy (DCM) and many congenital heart diseases are also commonly found in the Great Dane, leading to its nickname of the Heartbreak breed, in conjunction with its shorter lifespan. Great Danes also suffer from several genetic disorders that are specific to the breed. For example, if a Great Dane lacks color (is white) near its eyes or ears then that organ does not develop and usually the dog will be either blind, deaf, or both.

Origins

It is reported that the Great Dane was developed from mastiff-like dogs taken to Germany by the Alans.

According to Barbara Stein, "The breed originated in Germany, probably from a cross between the English mastiff and the Irish Wolfhound." However, other sources maintain that the breed originated in Denmark and still others report the question as controversial and unsettled. In 1749 Georges-Louis Leclerc, Comte de Buffon used the name "le Grand Danois," (translated by William Smellie as "Great Dane"). Up until that time the hound was referred to in England as "Danish dog." According to Jacob Nicolay Wilse the Danes called the dog "large hound," a terminology continued well in to the 20th century. As late as in the 1780 Germany the hound is referred to as "Grosser Dänischer Jagdhund" (). At the first dog exhibition, held in Hamburg 14–20 July 1863, eight dogs were called "Dänische Dogge" and seven "Ulmer Doggen."

Great Danes in popular culture

- The Great Dane was named the state dog of Pennsylvania in 1965.
- Scooby-Doo, the famous Hanna-Barbera character, was based on a Great Dane by animation designer Iwao Takamoto. Takamoto based his illustrations on sketches given to him by a Hanna-Barbera employee who bred this dog. Scooby closely resembles a Great Dane, although his tail is longer than the breed's, bearing closer resemblance to a cat's tail.
- Damien The Great Dane has been the mascot of the University at Albany since 1965; In 2003, the school added Lil' D, a smaller Great Dane, to help Damien entertain the crowds.
- Brutus in *The Ugly Dachshund*, a Great Dane raised by a Dachshund mother.
- *Marmaduke* is a newspaper comic strip drawn by Brad Anderson from 1954 to the present day. The strip revolves around the Winslow family and their Great Dane, Marmaduke.
- In The Guardian (novel) by Nicholas Sparks the main but tragic hero is Singer, a Great Dane, acting as the guardian of a true love.

See also

- Argentine Dogo

External links

- AKC Great Dane Breed Standard [1]
- Breed Information Resource [2]
- The Great Dane Owners Forum and Information Resource [3]

Great Pyrenees

The **Pyrenean Mountain Dog**, known as the **Great Pyrenees** in the United States, is a large breed of dog, used as a livestock guardian dog.

The Great Pyrenees is a very old breed, and has been used for hundreds of years by shepherds, including those of the Basque people, who inhabit parts of the region in and around the Pyrenees Mountains of southern France and northern Spain. One of the first descriptions of the breed dates from 1407, and from 1675 the breed was a favourite of The Grand Dauphin and other members of the French aristocracy. By the early nineteenth century there was a thriving market for the dogs in mountain towns, from where they would be taken to other parts of France. However as late as 1874 the breed was not completely standardised in appearence, with two major sub-types recorded, the Western and the Eastern. They are related to several other large white European livestock guardian dogs (LGD), including the Italian Maremma Sheepdog, Kuvasz (Hungary), Akbash Dog (Turkey) and Polish Tatra or Polski Owczarek Podhalański.

Description

Males grow to and , while females reach and . They live to 10–12 years of age.

Their coats are white and can have varying shades of gray, red (rust), or tan around the face (including a full face mask), ears and sometimes on the body and tail. As Great Pyrenees mature, their coats grow thicker and the longer colored hair of the coat often fades on those dogs that were not born completely white. Sometimes a little light tan or lemon will appear later in life around the ears and face. Being a double-coated breed, the undercoat can also have color and the skin as well. The color of the nose and on the eye rims should be jet black. Grey or tan markings that remain lend the French name, "blaireau," (badger) which is a similar grizzled mixture color seen in the European badger. More recently, any color is correctly termed "Badger" or "Blaireau."

All white dogs are not preferred by top breeders for many reasons. White dogs in most breedings are less frequent. It's not unusual that breedings that result in a high incidence of all white puppies do not have the required jet black pigment on the nose and eye rims. These breeding lines are therefore not, as a rule, desirable in well-bred stock. There are generally all white puppies in most litters. This is normal and these all white puppies can be bred successfully in the hands of a competent breeder. The rear leg bilateral double dewclaws are required.

In popular culture

- In the anime/manga Azumanga Daioh, Chiyo Mihama's pet Tadakichi-san (Mr. Tadakichi) is a Great Pyrenees.
- Akamaru, the canine familiar of Kiba Inuzuka, in the anime/manga *Naruto* is based on many species of dogs including Great Pyrenees.
- In the novel, Belle et Sébastien and 60s children's TV series, Belle is a Great Pyrenees.
- The 2004 film *Finding Neverland* used a Great Pyrenees to represent J.M. Barrie's Landseer Newfoundland dog.
- The Spanish designer Javier Mariscal was inspired by this dog breed for the design of the 1992 Summer Olympics mascot "Cobi".
- In *Hanazakarino Kimitachihe*, the male lead had a Great Pyrenees named "Yu Ci Lan" for a pet.
- The Japanese series Ginga Densetsu Weed features a Great Pyrenees named Hiro, who is nicknamed the "ball snatcher", due to his signature attack of neutering his opponents.
- In the film "Those Magnificent Men in their Flying Machines" (1965), a Great Pyrenees is the household dog at the Lord Rawnsley estate.
- In the Marx Brothers' "Horse Feathers" a Great Pyrenees appears in the dog catcher's wagon.
- In the Korean variety show *Happy Sunday - 1 Night 2 Days*, Sang Geun is a Great Pyrenees.
- A popular Korean singer, Hero Jaejoong from TVXQ owns a Great Pyrenees named Vic.
- In the 2009 Disney movie Santa Buddies, a Great Pyrenees puppy named Puppy Paws is the leading character.
- In the Jim Carrey movie "Dumb and Dumber" a Great Pyrenees appears in the dog-mobile.
- In the manga/anime Fullmetal Alchemist the dog Alexander is a Great Pyrenees

See also

- Akbash Dog
- Argentine Dogo
- Kuvasz
- Mucuchies
- Maremma Sheepdog
- Polish Tatra Sheepdog
- Slovak Cuvac

External links

- GPCA [1] Great Pyrenees Club of America
- Great Pyrenees Community [2] The gathering place for everyone who has an interest in Great Pyrenees. Study groups, blogs, and much more with levels of interest for everyone.
- Great Pyrenees Library [3] : interesting and useful articles on breeding, behavior, livestock guardians, Great Pyrenees rescue and medical information
- GreatPyr.com [4] : Great Pyrenees Information & Resources. Photo Gallery, Forums, and Breed Information
- Great Pyrenees Connection [5]: Great Pyrenees breed information, photographs, history of the breed in France and the Netherlands, links to international Great Pyrenees breeders and Great Pyrenees clubs
- Livestock Guardian Dog Association [6]
- Movie about the characteristics of the Pyrenean Mountain Dog [7]*

Greater Swiss Mountain Dog

The **Greater Swiss Mountain Dog** or **Grosser Schweizer Sennenhund** or **Grand Bouvier Suisse** is a dog breed which was developed in the Swiss Alps, Switzerland. The name Sennenhund refers to people called *Senn* or Senner, dairymen and herders in the Swiss Alps. The dogs are almost certainly the result of mating of indigenous dogs with large Mastiff-type dogs brought to Switzerland by foreign settlers. At one time these dogs were believed to have been among the most popular dogs in Switzerland. The breed was assumed to have almost died out by the late 19th century, as their work was being done by other breeds or machines, but they were rediscovered in the early 1900s.

It is a large, heavy-boned dog with incredible physical strength. Despite being heavy-boned and well-muscled, the dog is agile enough to perform the all-purpose farm duties of the mountainous regions of its origin. The Greater Swiss Mountain Dog Standard calls for a black, white and rust colored coat. These are big dogs.

This breed is a sociable, active, calm and dignified dog, and loves being part of the family. This breed is relatively healthy for their size; Greater Swiss Mountain Dogs have far fewer problems than more popular breeds in the similar size range. The Greater Swiss Mountain Dog is considered the oldest of the four Swiss breeds. It is the largest of the four Sennenhund breeds; all four have the same colors and markings but are different sizes.

History

Breed history

The origin of the Greater Swiss Mountain Dog is not definitely known. The Swiss people themselves cannot be clearly defined as belonging exclusively to one of the European tribes; they are inhabitants of a typical transit country. Likewise, the Swiss mountain dogs are probably be the result of original farm dogs mating with passing dogs of warriors and travelers. For three centuries beginning in 1515, the remote valleys of Switzerland were more or less isolated from world history, and specific breeds of dogs were created by inbreeding – puppies were given to neighbors and family members.

The Greater Swiss Mountain Dog was developed in the Swiss Alps, Switzerland; there are several theories regarding the origins of the Swiss Sennenhund breeds. The most popular theory states the dogs are descended from the Molossian, a large Mastiff-type dog, which accompanied the Roman Legions on their invasion of the Alps more than 2000 years ago.

A second theory is that about 1100 B.C. the Phoenicians brought a large breed of dog with them to settlements in Spain, and that these dogs later migrated eastward to influence the development of the Spanish Mastiff, Great Pyrenees, Dogue de Bordeaux and large Swiss breeds.

A third possibility is that a large breed was indigenous to central Europe back in the Neolithic Period – when humans used wild and domestic crops, as well as domesticated animals. Whether or not a domesticated large breed existed in the Alpine area when the Romans invaded, Greater Swiss Mountain Dogs are almost certainly the result of the mating of indigenous dogs with large Mastiff-type dogs brought to Switzerland by foreign settlers. The early ancestors of the Greater Swiss Mountain Dog were used by farmers, herdsmen and merchants in central Europe. The breed was bred as a draft dog to pull heavy carts, to guard and move dairy cattle, and as a watchdog and family companion.

Selective breeding

Selective breeding was based on a dog's ability to perform a particular function, such as pulling loads or guarding. The Swiss farmer needed a strong, multi-purpose dog capable of contributing to daily life on the farm. Large, sturdy and confident, the Greater Swiss Mountain Dog is a draft and drover breed – robust and agile enough to perform farm work in very mountainous regions. The breed was also used as a butcher's dog; the breed had been "popular with butchers, cattle dealers, manual workers and farmers, who used them as guard dogs, droving or draught dogs and bred them as such." The breed is a very alert, strong and athletic dog who can out-power most breeds of dog. Their popularity as a draft dog led to the nickname, "the poor man's horse." By the 19th century, the ancestors of the modern Greater Swiss Mountain Dog were widely used in central Europe by farmers and tradesmen.

Renewal of breed

Prevailing theory

Most of the breed standard sources and other sources have the information in this section about the history of the Greater Swiss Mountain Dog's rescue from extinction.

At one time these dogs were believed to have been among the most popular dogs in Switzerland. The breed was assumed to have almost died out by the late 19th century, as their work was being done by other breeds or machines, but they were rediscovered in the early 1900s.

On the 25th anniversary of the founding of the Swiss Kennel Club (Schweizerische Kynologische Gesellschaft or SKG) in 1908, two short-haired Bernese Mountain Dogs were shown by Franz Schertenlieb (also spelled Schertenleib) to an advocate of the Swiss mountain dogs, geology Professor Albert Heim (April 12, 1849 – August 31, 1937). Heim recognized them as representatives of the old, vanishing, large mountain dog, whose ancestors had been widely spread across Europe, and bred as guard-, draught- and droving-cattle dogs.

Heim was an expert of Sennenhund breeds, and began to encourage breeders to take an interest in them; his efforts resulted in the re-establishment of the breed. The dogs were recognised as a separate breed by the SKG in 1909 and entered as "Grosser Schweizer Sennenhund" in Volume 12 of the Swiss stud book. The first breed club was formed in 1912 to promote this breed and keep it purebred. The Bernese Mountain Dog and the Greater Swiss Mountain Dog are two of four distinctive farm-type dogs of Swiss origin who were saved from extinction and revitalized by the Schertenlieb in the late 1800s.

Another theory

There is no written information about the Greater Swiss Mountain Dog before 1907; he did not exist as a breed. Until 1913 written mention is only in reports by exhibition judges; written mainly by Professor Dr. Albert Heim, who is credited with introducing them into official dog breeding. Heim was sure that the Greater Swiss Mountain Dog was the most widely kept dog in the mountain areas of Switzerland between 1860 and 1870. By the end of the century the breed is supposed to have disappeared. Hans Raber doubts the dog would have disappeared by 1900. If this dog was common around 1870, it is difficult to believe that 30 years later it could be found only in remote Bern valleys. A well-known and working dog cannot disappear in such a short time, especially if he had the good qualities he was known for.

Systematic breeding did not occur. It is difficult to imagine that a farmer would take his in-season female to a specially selected male; breeding was left to chance. From the litter – Swiss Mountain dogs can have litters of up to 18 puppies – those who were likeable and looked suitable were chosen. Because of strict selection and puppies that were normally kept in the neighborhood, there was a stability in resemblance and character. Practical use dictated appearance; the dog had to have an impressive size, he had to tolerate bad weather, be of steady temperament and not eat too much. It isn't known how much attention was given to colors; it could be that the evenly marked, or the tri-colored dog was preferred over the irregularly marked dog.

Heim says that the big butcher dogs − Metzgerhund − disappeared when foreign dogs were imported. Raber questions if farmers would get a foreign dog, especially if it cost money. The Swiss mountain dog could not have disappeared by 1900. Heim does not answer to what kind of dog farmers used in 1900; he mentions mongrels − the Sennenhunde in 1860 were mongrels. In 1889 an International Dog Show was held in Winterthur, northern Switzerland; various Sennenhunds were exhibited. Raber is sure the dogs were present in 1900 as draft dogs for peddlers and people going to market, watch dogs for farmers and drover's dog for butchers; they were rarely tri-colored. Everywhere the dogs had short, rough coats; nearly all were brown, yellow or black with white and brown markings. Lons' description of the northern and central German butcher dog also fits the Sennenhunde at the beginning of pure breeding; this applies to the Austrian butcher dog of Linz, and the French and Belgian Matin. It is to their credit that Heim and Schertenleib selected one variation of the butcher dog − possible the most beautiful − and started it on the road to a pure breed.

In 1908 the Swiss mountain dog appeared for the first time in public. At a show in Langenthal, Switzerland, Franz Schertenleib − a breeder of the Berner − showed an extraordinarily strong, short-haired Berner Sennenhund. He had seen this dog and bought him as an oddity. He was eager to hear what the Langenthal judge, Professor Heim, would say about this short-haired Berner. Bello vom Schlossgut was beautifully marked, high, sturdy, and with attractive colors. Heim's first look saw the possibility of a new breed of Sennenhunde. He remembered having seen similar dogs in the 1860s in various parts of Switzerland. He said to Schertenleib, "The dog belongs in a different category; he is too gorgeous and thoroughbred to push him aside as a poor example of a Berner. He is an example of the old-time, almost extinct, butcher dog." Heim wrote in his judge's notes: "Bello is a marvelous, old Sennen (Butcher) hund of the large, almost extinct breed. Had he been entered under "other breeds" I would have recognized him as grossen Sennenhund and awarded him first prize with pleasure. Since he was entered among the Durrbachs, I cannot give this interesting dog more than second prize. This dog is out of place here."

Heim gave Bello the name Grosse Schweizer Sennenhund and dismissed the first representative of a newly named breed from the ring. Heim wrote the first standard based on Bello, and Schertenleib started to search for other members of the new breed. He found two short-haired bitches and breeding began. The first Greater Swiss Mountain Dogs were stockier and rougher than the modern dogs; the skulls were wider than desirable today and showed a marked stop. Judging from old pictures, the coloring was bad; the black coat was mixed with yellow wool at the neck, flanks and rear.

Development in the 20th century

Throughout the early 20th century, the Greater Swiss Mountain Dog population in Europe grew slowly, and it remains a rare breed both in its native Switzerland and the U.S. During World War II the breed was used by the Swiss Army as a draft dog. In 1945 over 100 puppies were registered, indicating the existence of about 350-400 dogs of the breed at that time.

The breed was first recognised internationally in 1939, when the Swiss Standard was first published by the Fédération Cynologique Internationale. In 1968 J. Frederick and Patricia Hoffman imported the first Greater Swiss Mountain Dogs to the U.S. The Greater Swiss Mountain Dog Club of America was formed; the club promotes careful, selective breeding to gradually increase the strength and popularity of the breed. In 1983 the club held the first Greater Swiss Mountain Dog Club of America (GSMDCA) National Specialty; the club registry contained 257 dogs. In 1985 the breed was granted entrance to the American Kennel Club (AKC) Miscellaneous Group. In 1992 the GSMDCA started to work toward full AKC recognition, and in July 1995 the Greater Swiss Mountain Dog was officially granted full recognition in the AKC Working Group.

Appearance

The Greater Swiss Mountain Dog is a draft and drover breed; it is a large, heavy-boned dog with incredible physical strength. Despite being heavy-boned and well-muscled, the dog is agile enough to perform the all-purpose farm duties of the mountainous regions of its origin.

Coat

There is black on top of the dog's back, ears, tail and the majority of the legs. There should be rust on the cheeks, a thumb print above the eyes, and also rust should appear on the legs between the white and black. There should be white on the muzzle, the feet, the tip of the tail, on the chest, and up from the muzzle to pass between the eyes. Symmetrical markings are preferred by breeders.

The double coat has a dense outer coat of about long. Textures of the topcoat can range from short, straight and fine to longer, wavier and coarser. The under coat is thick and ranges from the preferred dark gray to light gray to tawny, and must be on the neck, but can be all over the body − with such an thick coat, Sennenhund shed throughout the year and they have a major shedding once or twice a year.

While the Greater Swiss Mountain Dog Standard calls for a black, white and rust dog; they do come in other colors which include blue, white and tan tri-color; and rust and white bi-color. On the blue tri-color dogs, blue replaces where black would be and tan replaces where the rust would normally be. On the rust bi-color dogs, the dog is solid rust and white markings with a total absence of black coloring.

Size

Males range between at the shoulder and females range between at the shoulder. There is no standard for weight in the Greater Swiss Mountain Dog; males tend to range between and females range between . Body length to height is approximately a 10 to 9 proportion; they are slightly longer than tall.

Conformation

Head

Greater Swiss Mountain Dogs have an animated and gentle expression. Their eyes are almond shaped, vary in color from hazel to chestnut − dark brown is preferred − medium-sized, and neither deep set nor protruding. Eyelids are close fitting and eyerims are black.

The medium-sized ears are set high, triangular in shape, gently rounded at the tip and hang close to the head when relaxed. When alert, the ears are brought forward and raised at the base. The top of the ear is level with the top of the skull.

The skull is flat and broad with a slight stop. The backskull and muzzle are approximately equal in length; the backskull is approximately twice the width of the muzzle. The muzzle is large, blunt and straight, and most often has a slight rise before the end. In adult dogs the nose leather is always black.

The lips are clean and as a dry-mouthed breed, flews are only slightly developed. They should not drool. The teeth meet in a scissors bite.

Neck, Topline and Body

The neck is of moderate length, strong, muscular and clean. The topline is level from the withers to the croup − the croup is the fused sacral vertebrae that form the roof of the pelvis and the first few vertebrae of the tail. The croup is long, broad and smoothly rounded to the tail insertion. The tail is thicker at the base, tapering to a point as it reaches the hocks; it is carried down in repose. When alert and in movement, the tail may be carried higher and curved slightly upward; it should not curl over the back. The bones of the tail should be straight.

The chest is deep and broad with a slightly protruding breastbone, with well-sprung ribs. The depth of the chest is approximately one-half the height of the dog at the withers, and the deepest point of the chest should lie between the elbows, not above them.

Forequarters

The shoulders of a Greater Swiss Mountain Dog are long, sloping, strong, moderately laid back, flat and well-muscled. Their forelegs are straight and strong.

A dog walks on its toes like a horse does; a dog's pastern and paws are analogous to the back of a human's hand and fingers, respectfully. The pasterns slope very slightly, but are not weak. Feet are round and compact with well-arched toes; the feet turn neither in nor out.

Hindquarters

The thighs are broad, strong and muscular; broad, strong and muscular hindquarters, and proper angles between the stifles and hocks are essential for a draft dog to provide powerful rear-drive during movement. The breed standard 'bend of stifle' refers to where the upper and the lower thighs meet. The stifles are moderately bent and taper smoothly into the hocks. The hocks are well let down and straight when viewed from the rear. The hock joint corresponds to the human ankle and first short bones in the foot; the dog does not walk on the heel as people do. Feet are round and compact with well-arched toes; they turn neither in nor out. Dewclaws should be removed.

Gait

The gait of the Greater Swiss Mountain Dog should have movement with a level back. Their gait should have good reach in front with a powerful drive in the rear. Soundness, balance and efficiency which accompany correct structure and good condition are crucial factors in their movement, not speed. Greater Swiss Mountain Dogs were bred to work all day on a farm and need stamina. They are a large breed; because of their history as farm dogs in mountainous terrain, they are extremely agile and this is apparent in their gait.

Temperament

The Greater Swiss Mountain Dog is happy with an enthusiastic nature and strong affinity to people and children. This breed is sociable, active, calm and dignified. They do need plenty of room to exercise. They will not be happy confined to kennel life; they want to enjoy their family. They crave attention and physical contact. Greater Swiss Mountain Dogs are bold, faithful and willing workers and are eager to please. The Greater Swiss Mountain Dog is confident in nature; the breed is gentle with children. He can be stubborn and determined. The Greater Swiss Mountain Dog is an intelligent breed and is a quick learner. He can be difficult to housebreak, and tends to try and eat just about anything, edible or not.

The activity level in the Greater Swiss Mountain Dog is variable. They are capable of being athletic, but usually that activity is in bursts; they are active for short periods of time followed by napping. They want to be with their owners and to participate; their activity level most often matches the activity level of the family. As a working dog, they like having a job to do and enjoy participating in hiking, carting, obedience trials, herding, weight pulling and backpacking with their owners.

Being alert and vigilant, the Greater Swiss Mountain Dog is a good watchdog. They tend to notice everything in their surroundings and are quick to sound alarm. Faced with a threat they will stand their ground and put on a show that will intimidate those unfamiliar with the dog. Greater Swiss Mountain Dogs are accepting of a non-threatening stranger. They are confident and comfortable in unfamiliar locations, and are stable around strange noises and unfamiliar people. They are accepting of other dogs and species, and are reluctant to bite.

This giant breed matures slowly in both mind and body, taking anywhere from 2 to 3 years. The objective in training this dog is for the owner to achieve pack leader status. As youngsters, they can be quite boisterous and they do require steady and reliable training to develop manners and physical self-control. As with all large, active working dogs this breed should be well socialized early in life with other dogs and people, and be provided with regular activity and training.

Health

For the most part, this breed is relatively healthy for their size; Greater Swiss Mountain Dogs have far fewer problems than more populous breeds in the similar size range.

Urinary Incontinence

Urinary Incontinence (UI) is defined as involuntary urination, and most often occurs in Greater Swiss Mountain Dogs as leaking of urine while sleeping; it is a non-life threatening condition. It seems that more than 20% of the females are affected, usually after being spayed. Incontinence is occasionally found in males as well. Incontinence can occur for many reasons, such as a weak bladder sphincter – generally the most common cause in Greater Swiss Mountain Dogs – urinary tract infection, excessive water consumption, congenital structural defects and spinal cord disease.

Eyelash issues

The two most common eye issues that Greater Swiss Mountain Dogs face are distichiasis and entropian, with distichiasis being the most common issue. Distichiasis is the presence of extra eyelashes along the eyelid. Distichiasis has been reported in 19%, of the breed and in the vast majority of cases it is non-symptomatic and does not cause an issue for the dog. Extra eyelashes can be seen along the eyelid; sometimes extra eyelashes grow so that they irritate the eye. Treatment varies from vet to vet, some choosing to freeze the affected hair follicles and others choosing to use electrocautery.

Entropian – found in about 3% of the breed – is the rolling in of the eyelids, which causes the eyelashes to irritate the eye. Entropian is a condition that often requires surgery to fix, but once corrected causes no future issues for the dog.

Lick fit

Lick fit is a term use to describe the frantic licking that Greater Swiss Mountain Dogs can be prone to. This has been reported in 17% of the breed. When in the middle of a lick fit, the dog will lick anything they can – carpet, floors, walls – and will eat anything they can find – grass, leaves, dirt, carpet – and will gulp air and swallow constantly. Their actions make it obvious they are in severe gastrointestinal discomfort. Many owners are able to prevent lick fits by ensuring the dog never has an empty stomach by frequent, smaller meals and large dog biscuits as between meal snacks.

Epilepsy

Ideopathic Epilepsy (IE) is the condition of frequent seizures with no identifiable cause. Seizures occur when nerve cells in the brain become hyperexited and send rapid-fire messages to the body. Treatment of IE depends on the severity of the case and may involve daily administration of anticonvulsant drugs. IE is present in all Greater Swiss Mountain Dog lines; it typically surfaces between the ages of 1 to 3 years, but it can become evident as early as 12 months and as late as 5 years. The median age of death from epilepsy in the breed is 3.75 years. Canine genetics researcher, Dr. George Padgett, recently concluded that at least 39% of Greater Swiss Mountain Dogs carry the genes to produce epilepsy.

Abdominal health issues

Bloat – gastric dilitation-volvulous (GDV) – is the greatest killer of the Greater Swiss Mountain Dog. GDV occurs in deep-chested breeds and requires immediate veterinary care. It can be caused by wolfing down too much water, too much food too fast, exercise after eating, stress or unknown conditions. Symptoms are distended abdomen, excessive salivating, depression and lethargy. When bloat occurs it cuts off the esophagus, and blood supply to the heart is lessened causing low blood pressure as well as other cardiac problems; the dog can go into shock. Organ damage can occur as well and the stomach may rupture causing peritonitis to set in. If not treated, the dog may die.

The spleen is located in the left cranial abdomen and is held loosely in place by ligaments. Primary diseases of the spleen are splenic torsion and splenic tumors. Splenic torsion occurs when the spleen twists along the axis of the blood supply. Symptoms of splenic torsion include lethargy, abdominal distension and pale mucous membranes. One theory for the development of splenic torsion is that for dogs with chronic intermittent gastric dilatation, the dilation causes the spleen's ligaments to stretch and increases the spleen's mobility within the abdomen. The spleen becomes torsed because it is no longer anchored in its correct location. In a normal Greater Swiss Mountain Dog the spleen is smooth and uncreased; it is about by , and less than thick. Most of the spleens removed from Greater Swiss Mountain Dogs are by and very thick. This size spleen is not an abnormal finding in this breed. It seems apparent that many dogs of the breed suffer enlarged spleens for no obvious reason other than the spleen may have been constantly twisting, folding and unfolding.

Dysplasias

Canine Hip Dysplasia (CHD) is the irregular formation of the joint that joins the femur — the longest bone in the body — to the hip socket. The hip is a ball-and-socket joint and the femoral head must fit well into the socket for the joint to function properly. Early signs of CHD include a reluctance to go up and down stairs or to jump; difficulty rising or laying down; and bunny hopping when running — both hind limbs move together. CHD is among the principal orthopedic diseases in the Greater Swiss Mountain Dog; it is rarely severe and crippling. Unless x-rays are taken many owners are not aware that they have a dysplastic dog. A goal for raising a Greater Swiss Mountain Dog from puppyhood is to feed them so they mature more slowly than smaller breeds to help avoid hip and other orthopedic problems in adulthood.

The form of Canine Elbow Dysplasia most often diagnosed in Greater Swiss Mountain Dogs appears to be a degerative joint disease — a slowly progressive form of cartilage degeneration usually caused by trauma or abnormal wear on the joint. Evidence suggests that most dogs of this breed diagnosed with degenerative joint disease by x-rays of the elbows have the mildest form Grade I. They don't display clinical signs such as pain, stiffness, decreased range of motion or lameness.

Osteochondrosis is a disturbance in the normal development of cartilage; cartilage becomes abnormally thickened, and small fissures and cracks may develop. Dissecans is when cartilage becomes dissected resulting in cartilage flaps, which may remain attached or become loose and fall into the joint space. In Greater Swiss Mountain Dogs most of these cases occur in the shoulder joints and occasionally in elbows and hocks. Except for very mild cases without flap development, the clinical signs are persistent or intermittent lameness. The dog may be stiff after resting and the lameness is usually aggravated by exercise. It is diagnosed by x-rays, and treatment depends on the severity of the case. Mild cases without cartilage flaps may be treated and heal with several weeks of rest and treatment with medication and supplements. Many cases require surgery to remove the flaps and loose fragments, and scraping and smoothing of the defective surface. Surgical repair of the shoulder usually has excellent results, surgical results involving other sites are not as predictable.

Lifespan

Heavier dogs, such as the Greater Swiss Mountain Dogs, tend to have shorter lifespans than medium- and small-sized dogs; longevity is inversely related to breed size. Two web sites list the life expectancy for Greater Swiss Mountain Dogs at 10 to 11 years; another lists it as 8–10 years. Dog lifespans may vary in different countries, even in the same breed.

Kennel club and pet registry recognition

- The Grosser Schweizer Sennenhund, or Greater Swiss Mountain Dog, is recognised internationally by the Fédération Cynologique Internationale (FCI). They are in Group 2, Section 3 Swiss Mountain and Cattle Dogs; standards are dated March 25, 2003. The first standard was published not before February 5, 1939.

- The American Kennel Club (AKC) fully recognized the breed in 1995, and classifies them in the Working Group.

- The Canadian Kennel Club recognized the breed in 2006, and also places the breed in the Working Group.

- The United Kennel Club recognized the breed in 1992; they place the breed in the Guardian Dog Group.

- The Kennel Club, based in the United Kingdom, classifies the Greater Swiss Mountain Dog in the Working Group.

- The Continental Kennel Club (CKC) lists the Greater Swiss Mountain Dog and provides minimal information about the breed.

- The America's Pet Registry Inc. (APRI) does have a classified ad section for Greater Swiss Mountain Dogs.

- The American Canine Registry (ACR) lists the Greater Swiss Mountain Dog as an acceptable breed under their American Canine Registry section.

- As of May 2010 the breed is not recognised by the New Zealand Kennel Club or the Australian National Kennel Council.

Four breeds of Sennenhund

The Greater Swiss Mountain Dog is considered the oldest of the Swiss breeds. It is the largest of the four Sennenhund breeds; all four have the same colors and markings but are different sizes.

Evolutionary hierarchy suggests breeds should genetically cluster into groups sharing recent common ancestry. A genetic clustering algorithm could not easily distinguish between the obviously related pairs of Greater Swiss Mountain Dog and the Bernese Mountain Dog.

The four breeds of Sennenhund, with the original breed name followed by the most popular English version of the breed name, and their size:

- Grosser Schweizer Sennenhund, Greater Swiss Mountain Dog. Males range between at the shoulder and females range between at the shoulder. There is no standard for weight in the Greater Swiss Mountain Dog; males tend to weigh between and females weigh between .

- Berner Sennenhund, Bernese Mountain Dog. This is the only one of the four with a long coat; it is the second-largest with males at high and . Females are tall and weigh .

- Appenzeller Sennenhund, Appenzeller Mountain Dog. Males are tall and weighs . Females are tall.

- Entlebucher Sennenhund, Entlebucher Mountain Dog. Males are tall, and females are . They weigh .

Similar breeds

In addition to the three breeds mentioned in the previous section, Greater Swiss Mountain Dogs are related to other mountain dogs: Boxers, Bullmastiffs, Doberman Pinschers, Great Danes, Great Pyrenees, Komondors, Kuvaszes and Mastiffs. The breed probably contributed to the development of the St. Bernard and the Rottweiler.

See also

- Breed group (dog)
- Carting

External links

- Historical photos of the Grosser Schweizer Sennenhund [1] from the Berne Naturaidogsarebad History Museum
- More information about geologist and indigenous Swiss dog breeds advocate Albert Heim (1849-1937), including a photo with Swiss Mountain Dogs in 1929 [2] (in German)
- Genetics of tricolour coats [4], KG
- DMOZ links to more information about the Greater Swiss Mountain Dog [3]

Komondor

The **Komondor** (Hungarian plural *komondorok*) is a large white-colored Hungarian breed of livestock guardian dog with a long, corded coat. The Komondor is an old-established powerful dog breed which has a natural guardian instinct to guard livestock and other property. The Komondor was mentioned for the first time in 1544 in a Hungarian codex. The Komondor breed has been declared one of Hungary's national treasures, to be preserved and protected from modification.

The Puli is another Hungarian sheep dog about half the size of the Komondor, and usually black in color.

History

The origin of the Komondor is debated. Some believe the Komondor were a dog of the Magyars. According to the most probable explanation, Komondors were brought to Hungary by Cumans, the Turkish speaking, nomadic people who settled Hungary during the 12th and 13th century. The name Komondor is found for the first time written in 1544 in the History of King Astiagis by Kákonyi Péter, in Hungarian. Later in 1673 Amos Comenius mentions the Komondor in one of his works.

The unique dreadlock appearance gives a hint of common origin with the Puli and the Bergamasco. There might also be a link between the Komondor and the big, white Russian livestock dogs, the South Russian Ovcharka. The dreadlock coat must have developed under a dry and extreme temperature climate as it provides superb protection against cold and hot weather, but is not too comfortable in wet weather.

The Komondor is built for livestock guarding. It is big, strong, and armored with a thick coat. The coat provides protection against wild animals and the weather and vegetation, the coat of the dog looks similar to that of a sheep so it can easily blend into a flock and camouflage itself giving it an advantage when predators such as wolves attack. The coat is the trademark of the breed.

Today the Komondor is a fairly common breed in Hungary, its country of origin. Many Komondors were killed during World War II and local stories say that this is because the dog had to be killed before the building where it lived could be captured.

Description

Appearance

The Komondor is a large dog (many are over 30 inches tall), making this one of the largest common breeds of dog, or a molosser. The body is covered by a heavy, matted, corded coat. The dogs have robust bodies, strongly muscled, with long legs and a short back, with the tails carried low. The body, seen sideways, forms a prone rectangle. The length of body is slightly longer than the height at the withers, approximately 104% of the height at withers.

The Komondor has a broad head with the muzzle slightly shorter than half of the length of the head, with an even and complete scissor bite. Nose and lips are always black. People unfamiliar with the breed are often surprised by how quick and agile the dogs are.

The minimum height of female Komondors is at the withers, with an average height of . The minimum height of male Komondors is with an average height of . No upper height limit is given. Komondor females on average weigh between and Komondor males weigh on average between .

Coat

The Komondor's coat is a long, thick, strikingly corded white coat, about $20 - 27$ cm long (the heaviest amount of fur in the canine world), which resembles dreadlocks or a mop. The puppy coat is soft and fluffy. However, the coat is wavy and tends to curl as the puppy matures. A fully mature coat is formed naturally from the soft undercoat and the coarser outer coat combining to form tassels, or cords and will take around two years to form. Some help is needed in separating the cords so the dog does not turn into one large matted mess. The length of the cords increases with time as the coat grows. Shedding is very minimal with this breed, contrary to what one might think (once cords are fully formed). The only substantial shedding occurs as a puppy before the dreadlocks fully form. The Komondor is born with only a white coat, unlike the similar-looking Puli, which can be white, black, or sometimes grayish. However, a working Komondor's coat may be discolored by the elements, and may appear off-white if not washed regularly. Traditionally the coat protected the Komondor from wolves' bites, as the bites were not able to penetrate the thick coat. The coat of the Komondor takes about two and a half days to dry after a bath.

Temperament

The Komondor's temperament is like that of most livestock guarding dogs; it is calm and steady when things are normal, but in case of trouble, the dog will fearlessly defend its charges. It was bred to think and act independently and make decisions on his own.

It is affectionate with its family, and gentle with the children and friends of the family. Although wary of strangers, they can accept them when it is clear that no harm is meant, but is instinctively very protective of its family, home and possessions. The Komondor is good with other family pets but is intolerant to trespassers and teasing, and is not a good dog for city life. The dog is vigilant, will rest in the daytime, keeping an eye on the surroundings, but at night is constantly moving, patrolling the place, moving up and down around the whole area. The dogs usually knock down intruders and keep them down until the owner arrives. Hungarian Komondor breeders used to say that an intruder may be allowed to enter the property guarded by a Komondor, but he will not be allowed to come out again.

Uses

The breed has a natural guardian instinct and ability to guard livestock. An athletic dog, the Komondor is fast and powerful and will leap at a predator to drive it off or knock it down. It can be used successfully to guard sheep against wolves or bears. The Komondor is one breed of livestock guardian dog which has seen a vast increase in use as a guardian of sheep and goats in the United States to protect against predators such as coyotes, cougars, bears, and other predators.

Training

Due to the Komondor's size, power, speed and temperament, a lack of obedience training, which should start from a young age (4 − 8 months), can result in danger to others. Komondors generally take well to training if started early. A Komondor can become obstinate when bored, so it is imperative that training sessions be upbeat and happy. Praise is a must, as are consistent and humane corrections. Once a Komondor gets away with unfriendly or hostile behavior, it will always think such behavior is appropriate. Therefore, consistent corrections even with a young puppy are necessary to ensure a well-adjusted adult. Socialization is also extremely important. The Komondor should be exposed to new situations, people and other dogs as a puppy. Because it is a natural guard dog, a Komondor that is not properly socialized may react in an excessively aggressive manner when confronted with a new situation or person.

Given the proper environment and care, a Komondor is a responsible, loving dog. They are devoted and calm without being sluggish. As in any breed, there is quite a range of personalities, so your needs should be outlined clearly to your breeder. An experienced breeder can try to identify that personality which would be happier as an independent livestock dog, or that which wants more to please and would make a good obedience dog or family pet. Adolescence can be marked by changes in a Komondor's temperament, eating habits, trainability and general attitude. Many Komondors are "late bloomers," not fully mature until nearly three years of age.

Health

Komondors do not suffer many hereditary problems. Perhaps because the breed has descended from centuries of hardy working stock, Komondors have few genetically linked problems. In particular, there is no evidence of the retinal eye problems found in other breeds, nor is there dwarfism or hereditary blood disorders.

Hip dysplasia

As in all large breeds (and some small ones) there is some hip dysplasia, though the incidence is about 10% of all radiographs submitted, according to statistical studies of the OFA.

Eyes

There are two eye disorders found in the breed. Entropion is indicated by the curling inwards of either the upper or lower eyelid. This lid deformity causes the lashes to rub against the cornea causing lacerations and infections. More recently, juvenile cataracts have been documented. The Canine Eye Registration Foundation, CERF, located at Purdue University, evaluates eye exams and assigns a CERF number to it if the dog's eyes are free from genetic problems.

Bloat

There is some indication of bloat, a life-threatening condition. The incidence of bloat is no greater than with any other large breeds. To possibly help to avoid bloat do not feed soon before or after any exercise.

Parasites

External parasites can be a problem due to the heavy coat. As with any long-haired dog, a skin check should be part of a regular grooming routine. If fleas or ticks are found, aggressive measures are in order. 'Spot-ons', shampoos and powders work well, but great care should be observed as it is easy to miss a spot where the fleas can hide. Owners should check anti-flea and tick preparations carefully with a veterinary surgeon as the Komondor can be extremely sensitive to some of these products. Be wary of over-the-counter treatments as these are often too weak to effectively treat infestation, others can cause severe reactions if dosed incorrectly. It is recommended to spot-test the coat before dipping as some flea dips have been known to discolor the white coat. Flea collars can also discolor the hair beneath them, so look for a white or transparent one.

Ears

Ear care should also be routine. As Komondors have ears which prevent air circulation, it is especially necessary to keep them clean and hair-free. Some ear canals are more hairy than others, but commercial powders, cleansing fluids and plucking of the hair can greatly reduce infections.

Feet

Thick hair grows between the pads of the feet which also requires maintenance. This hair can pick up burrs, or become a source of irritation and infection when wet. For the health and comfort of the dog, this hair should be cut out with an electric clipper or scissors to keep mats from forming between the foot pads.

Vaccinations

As in all breeds one should be careful that a Komondor have the proper vaccines against rabies, distemper, canine parvovirus, etc. Dogs should also be checked periodically for worms and other internal parasites. Like all stock guard dogs Komondors are usually extremely sensitive to anesthetics. These drugs should always be administered to effect, never by weight.

See also

• Bergamasco Shepherd
• Puli

External links

• Breed Standard [1] at the website of the American Kennel Club
• Komondor Club of America [2]
• Middle Atlantic States Komondor Club [3]
• The Komondor Club [4]
• Komondor pictures [5]

Kuvasz

The **Kuvasz** (, pl. **Kuvaszok**) is a dog breed of ancient Hungarian origin. Mention of the breed can be found in old Hungarian texts. It has historically been used to guard livestock, but has been increasingly found in homes as a pet over the last seventy years.

Description

Appearance

The Kuvasz is a large dog with a dense coat which is usually white in color and can range from wavy to straight in texture. Although the fur is white, the Kuvasz's skin pigmentation should be dark and the nose should be black. The eyes should have an almond shape. Females usually weigh between 35–50 kg (75-90 pounds) while males weigh between 50–70 kg (100-115 pounds) with a medium bone structure. The head should be half as wide as it is long with the eyes set slightly below the plane of the muzzle. The stop (where the muzzle raises to the crown of the head) should be defined but not abrupt. The precise standard varies by country. (See the Breed Standards for a more precise description.) To a casual observer, the Kuvasz may appear similar to a Great Pyrenees, Akbash, a Maremma Sheepdog, Samoyed or a white Poodle and Labrador Retriever mix. The Slovak Cuvac and the Polish Tatra Sheepdog are versions of the Kuvasz.

As with many livestock guardian dogs, the color of the Kuvasz's coat serves a functional purpose and is an essential breed criterion. Shepherds purposefully bred the Kuvasz to have a light colored coat so that it would be easier for the shepherds to distinguish the Kuvasz from wolves that would prey on the livestock during the night. The Komondor, a cousin of the Kuvasz, has a white coat for the same reason. Traditionally, the Hungarian Kuvasz's coat could be either white or cream colored with a wavy texture. However, there is some debate, particularly in the United States, concerning the appropriateness of "cream" colored coats in show-quality dogs and whether the coat should be straight or wavy in texture. Since washing and brushing out a coat, as done for shows in the US also causes the coat to appear straight, the debate may be circular. Straighter coats may also have appeared as the result of breeding programs that developed after World War II, when the breeding lines in Hungary were isolated from the rest of the world as a result of Soviet occupation (see History, below). By Hungarian standard the straight coat is not acceptable. There must be special twirls in the coat.

Temperament

The Kuvasz is a very intelligent dog and is often described as having a clownish sense of humor which can last throughout their adolescence and occasionally into adulthood. They are intensely loyal yet patient pets who appreciate attention but may also be somewhat aloof or independent, particularly with strangers. They rank 42nd in Stanley Coren's The Intelligence of Dogs. They require an experienced dog handler/trainer. In keeping with their origins as a livestock guardian, Kuvaszok are known to be fierce protectors of their families. Given their intelligence, constant awareness of their surroundings, as well as their size and strength, they can be quite impressive in this role. A Kuvasz should be courageous, disciplined and stable, while hyperactivity, nervousness and shyness are to be faulted.

The combination of intelligence, independence and protectiveness make obedience training and socialization necessities. Furthermore, despite their intelligence, they should not be perceived as easily trained. Their independent personalities can make training a difficult task which can wear on the patience of even experienced owners. As a result, they are not recommended for novices and those who do not have time to train and socialize them properly. An adolescent Kuvasz should be able to learn basic obedience commands and consistently respond to them; however the instinctive need to investigate strangers and protect its owner may cause the Kuvasz to act independently when off leash and ignore the calls of a frustrated handler. Finally, a potential owner should refrain from purchasing a Kuvasz if barking will be a problem at the home. While not all Kuvaszok are prone to barking, many of them fulfill their guardian role by vocally warning off potential threats, both real and imagined. On the other hand, many of these qualities make the Kuvasz excellent guardians for sheep or large estates. The Kuvasz has a very special, close connection to his owner.

History

Although regarded today as one of the Hungarian breeds, the Kuvasz's origins actually lay with a nomadic tribe and may have its true origins from Mesopotamia along with domestic sheep and goats. Around 2000 B.C., the Magyar tribes moved along the recently established trade routes of the steppes, gradually leading them to the Carpathian Basin in Hungary which they conquered in 896 A.D. With them came Kuvasz-type dogs, which primarily served as livestock guardians. In 1978, the fossilized skeleton of a 9th Century Kuvasz-type dog was discovered in Fenékpuszta near Keszthely, a discovery which was remarkable in that the morphology of the skeleton was almost identical to a modern Kuvasz. If accurate, such a discovery would mark the Kuvasz as among the oldest identifiable dog breeds as only a few breeds can be dated beyond the 9th Century.

After the Magyar settlement of the Carpathian Basin, the tribes converted to a more agrarian lifestyle and began to devote more resources towards animal husbandry. Whereas the Komondor was used in the lower elevations with drier climates, the Kuvasz was used in the wet pastures of the higher mountains and both were an integral part of the economy. Later, during the 15th Century, the Kuvasz became a highly prized animal and could be found in the royal court of King Matthias Corvinus.

Kuvasz puppies were given to visiting dignitaries as a royal gift, and the King was said to have trusted his dogs more than his own councilors. After the king's death, the popularity of the breed among the nobles waned but it was still frequently found in its traditional role of protecting livestock.

By the end of World War II, nearly all the Kuvaszok in Hungary had been killed. The dogs had such a reputation for protecting their families that they were actively sought and killed by German and Soviet soldiers, while at the same time some German police used to take Kuvaszok home with them. After the Soviet invasion and the end of the war, the breed was nearly extinct in Hungary. After the war, it was revealed that fewer than thirty Kuvaszok were left in Hungary and some sources indicate the number may have been as few as twelve. Since then, due to many dedicated breeders, Kuvaszok have repopulated Hungary. However, as a result of this near extinction, the genetic pool available to breeders was severely restricted and there is conjecture that some may have used other breeds, such as the Great Pyrenees, to continue their programs. The issue is further clouded by the need to use a classification of B pedigrees at the time to rebuild the breed.

Possible origins of the breed name

The word most likely comes from the Turkic word *kavas* meaning guard or soldier or *kuwasz* meaning protector. A related theory posits that the word may have originated from the ancient farmers of Russia, the Chuvash, who nurtured the breed for generations and contributed many words to the Hungarian language.

Grooming

The Kuvasz's stiff, dense coat, growing up to 15 cm (6 inches) in length, does not require any special grooming. It needs to be brushed once a week or, better still, every two or three days. For standard grooming purposes, use of a grooming rake or a pin-brush with rounded pins is recommended. To remove stubborn knots, use a curry comb or a large-toothed comb. During the spring and autumn the Kuvasz moults (also known as shedding), and he will lose copious amounts of hair very quickly. Frequent brushing is therefore needed to keep his coat tidy. A Kuvasz should not smell or have an odor; such is usually a sign of illness or a poor diet.

Health

Although generally a healthy and robust breed which can be expected to live approximately 12–14 years, Kuvaszok are prone to developmental bone problems. Accordingly, owners should take care to provide proper nutrition to their Kuvasz puppy and avoid subjecting the puppy to rough play. As with many large breeds, hip dysplasia, a painful and potentially debilitating condition, is not uncommon. Good genetics and proper nutrition as a puppy are key to avoiding these complications.

A Kuvasz puppy should not be fed a diet high in calories or protein as such diets have been associated with the development of orthopedic disorders later in life. The Kuvasz has a very efficient metabolism and is predisposed to rapid growth—vitamin supplements are not necessary and, in fact, should be avoided. Cooked bones should never be given to a Kuvasz or any other dog because the cooking process renders the bone brittle and prone to splintering, which can cause serious injury to the dog's mouth and digestive tract.

Gallery

Similar Breeds

- Italian Abruzzese Sheepdog
- French Great Pyrenees
- Slovakian Cuvac
- Turkish Akbash Dog
- Polish Tatra Sheepdog

References

Notations

- Hódosi, József, ed. *A Kuvasz*. Hungaria Kuvasz Klub, 1996. English Translation by International Kuvasz Book Project.

External links

- Kuvasz Breed Standard [1] at the website of the American Kennel Club

Breed Clubs

- Kuvasz Fanciers of America [2]
- Kuvasz Club of Canada [3]
- Kuvasz Club of America [4]
- Kuvasz Club of Canada [3]
- American Kuvasz Association [5]
- Kuvasz Information (includes extensive history) [6]

English Mastiff

The **English Mastiff**, referred to by virtually all Kennel Clubs simply as the **Mastiff**, is a large breed of dog descended from the ancient Alaunt through the Pugnaces Britanniae.

Appearance

With a massive body, broad skull and head of generally square appearance, it is one of the largest dog breeds in terms of mass. Though the Irish Wolfhound and Great Dane are taller, they are not nearly as robust.

The body is large with great depth and breadth, especially between the forelegs, causing these to be set wide apart. The AKC standard height (per their website) for this breed is at the shoulder for males and (minimum) at the shoulder for females. A typical male can weigh , a typical female can weigh .

The former standard specified the coat should be short and close-lying (though long haired Mastiffs, called "Fluffies", are occasionally seen) and the color is apricot-fawn, silver-fawn, fawn, or dark fawn-brindle, always with black on the muzzle, ears, and nose and around the eyes. (See **Coat Colour Inheritance** below.)

The greatest weight ever recorded for a dog by the Guinness Book of World Records was for a Mastiff from England named Zorba (1989), at over . Zorba stood at the shoulder and was from the tip of his nose to the tip of his tail. Zorba set this record in November 1989, when he was 8 years old, and about the size of a small donkey.

Coat colour inheritance

The colours of the Mastiff coat are differently described by various kennel clubs, but are essentially fawn or apricot, or those colours as a base for black brindle. A black mask should occur in all cases. The fawn is generally a light "silver" shade, but may range up to a golden yellow. The apricot may be a slightly reddish hue up to a deep, rich red. The brindle markings should ideally be heavy, even and clear stripes, but may actually be light, uneven, patchy, faint or muddled. Pied Mastiffs occur rarely. Other non-standard colours include black, blue brindle, and chocolate mask. Some Mastiffs have a heavy shading caused by dark hairs throughout the coat or primarily on the back and shoulders. Brindle is dominant over solid colour. Apricot is dominant over fawn, though that dominance may be incomplete. Most of the colour faults are recessive, though black is so rare in the Mastiff that it cannot be certain if it is recessive, or a mutation that is dominant.

Temperament

The Mastiff breed has a desired temperament, which is reflected in all formal standards and historical descriptions. Though calm and affectionate to its master, it is capable of protection. If an unfamiliar person approaches near the Mastiff's perceived territory or its master, ideally, it will immediately position itself between its master and the stranger. If the approaching person is perceived as a threat, the Mastiff may take immediate defensive action. Mastiffs are normally good natured, calm, easygoing, and surprisingly gentle for their size. It is a well-mannered house pet, provided it gets daily exercise and activity. The Mastiff is typically an extremely loyal breed, exceptionally devoted to its family and good with children and small dogs.

Health

The Mastiff is a particularly large dog demanding correct diet and exercise. Excessive running is not recommended for the first two years of the dog's life. However, regular exercise must be maintained throughout the dog's life in order to discourage slothful behavior and to prevent a number of health problems. A soft surface is recommended for the dog to sleep on in order to prevent the development of calluses, arthritis, and hygroma (an acute inflammatory swelling). Due to the breed's large size, puppies may potentially be smothered or crushed by the mother during nursing. A whelping box, along with careful monitoring can prevent such accidents. The expected lifespan is about 7 to 14 years.

Major issues can include hip dysplasia and gastric torsion. Minor problems include obesity, osteosarcoma, and cystinuria. Problems only occasionally found include cardiomyopathy, allergies, vaginal hyperplasia, cruciate ligament rupture, hypothyroidism, OCD, entropion, progressive retinal atrophy (PRA), and persistent pupillary membranes (PPM).

When purchasing a purebred Mastiff, experts often suggest that the dog undergo tests for hip dysplasia, elbow dysplasia, thyroid, and DNA for PRA.

History before the First World War

The Pugnaces Britanniae (Latin) was the name given by the Romans to the original English Mastiff.

For some, the Mastiff name probably evolved from the Anglo-Saxon word "masty", meaning "powerful". Other sources, like the Oxford English dictionary, say the word originated from the Old French word *mastin* (Modern French *mâtin*), the word being itself derived from Vulgar Latin *ma(n)suetinus* "tame", see Classical Latin *mansuetus* with same meaning.

In 1631, Conrad Heresbach referred to "the Mastie that keepeth the house". The Mastiff is descended from the ancient dogs brought to Britain by ancient traders and is recognized as the oldest British breed. It has been speculated that the Mastiff might have been brought to Britain by the Phoenicians in the 6th century BC. It was used in the blood sports of bear-baiting, bull-baiting, dog fighting, and lion-baiting. Dogs known as Bandogs, who were tied (bound) close to houses, were of Mastiff type.

They were described by John Caius in 1570 as vast, huge, stubborn, ugly, and eager, of a heavy and burdensome body. Throughout its history, the Mastiff has contributed to the development of a number of dog breeds.

When in 1415 Sir Peers Legh was wounded in the Battle of Agincourt, his Mastiff stood over and protected him for many hours through the battle. The Mastiff was later returned to Legh's home and was the foundation of the Lyme Hall Mastiffs. Five centuries later this pedigree figured prominently in founding the modern breed. Other aristocratic seats where Mastiffs are known to have been kept are Elvaston Castle (Charles Stanhope, 4th Earl of Harrington and his ancestors) and Chatsworth House. The owner of the Chatsworth Mastiffs (which were said to be of Alpine stock) was William Cavendish, 5th Duke of Devonshire, known to his family as Canis. Mastiffs were also kept at Hadzor Hall, owned by members of the Galton family, famous for industrialists and scientists, including Charles Darwin.

Some evidence exists that the Mastiff first came to America on the Mayflower, but the breed's documented entry to America did not occur until the late 1800s.

In 1835, the Parliament of the United Kingdom implemented an Act called the Cruelty to Animals Act 1835, which prohibited the baiting of animals. This may have led to decline in Mastiffs used for this purpose, but Mastiffs continued to be used as guards for country estates and town businesses. Organised breeding began in the 19th century, when J.W.(John Wigglesworth)Thompson sought out a bitch, Dorah, from John Crabtree, the head gamekeeper of Kirklees Hall, whose dogs were often in the name of his employer, Sir George Armitage. Dorah was descended in part from animals owned by Thompson's grandfather, Commissioner Thompson, at the beginning of the century, as well as a Mastiff of the Bold Hall line, recorded from 1705, one purchased from boatmen and another caught by Crabtree in a fox trap. J. W. Thompson's first stud dog Hector came from crossing a bitch, Juno, bought from animal dealer Bill George, to a dog, Tiger, owned by a Captain Fenton. Neither of these had any pedigree, as was normal for the period. Between 1830 and 1850 he bred the descendants of these dogs and some others to produce a line with the short, broad head and massive build he favoured. In 1835, T.V.H.Lukey started his operations by breeding an Alpine Mastiff bitch of the Chatsworth line, Old Bob-Tailed Countess (bought from dog dealer Bill White), to Pluto, a large black Mastiff of unknown origin belonging to the Marquis of Hertford. The result was a bitch called Yarrow, who was mated to Couchez, another Alpine Mastiff belonging (at the time) to White and later mated to a brindle dog also in White's possession. Lukey produced animals that were taller but less massive than Thompson's. After 1850, Thompson and Lukey collaborated, and the modern Mastiff was created, though animals without pedigree or of dubious pedigree continued to be bred from into the 20th century. Another important contribution to the breed was made by a dog called Lion, owned by Captain Garnier. He bought two Mastiffs from the previously mentioned dealer Bill George. The bitch, Eve, bought by George at Leadenhall Market, was old enough to be gray-muzzled, but of good type; the dog, Adam, was of reputed Lyme Hall origin, but bought at Tattersalls and suspected by Garnier of containing a "dash of Boarhound", an ancestral form of Great Dane. Garnier took them to the United States with him and brought back their puppy, Lion. He was bred to Lukey's Countess to produce Governor, the source of all existing Mastiff lines. (Lion was also mated to Lufra, a Scottish Deerhound, and their puppy Marquis appears in the pedigrees of both Deerhounds and Irish Wolfhounds.)

In the 1880s soundness was sacrificed for type (widely attributed to the short-headed but straight-stifled Ch. Crown Prince), and subsequently, the Mastiff lost popularity. In the USA particularly, Mastiffs declined steadily through the 1890s and the early twentieth century. From 1906 to 1918, only 24 Mastiffs were registered in the United States, none American bred after 1910. By the time the First World War ended, other than for a few imports, the breed was extinct outside of Great Britain.

History after the First World War

In 1918, a dog called Beowulf, bred in Canada from British imports Priam of Wingfied and Parkgate Duchess, was registered by the AKC, starting a slow re-establishment of the breed in North America. Priam and Duchess, along with fellow imports Ch Weland, Thor of the Isles, Caractacus of Hellingly and Brutus of Saxondale, ultimately contributed a total of only two descendants who would produce further offspring, Buster of Saxondale and Buddy. There were, however, a number of other imports in the period between the wars and in the early days of the Second World War, and those whose descendants survive were 12 in number, meaning the North American contribution to the gene pool after 1945 consists of 14 Mastiffs. In the British Isles, virtually all breeding stopped due to the rationing of meat. After the war, such puppies as were produced mostly succumbed to canine distemper, for which no vaccine was developed until 1950. Only a single bitch puppy produced by the elderly stock that survived the war reached maturity, Nydia of Frithend, and her sire had to be declared a Mastiff by the Kennel Club, as his parentage was unknown, and he was thought by some to be a Bullmastiff. After the war, animals from North America, prominently from Canada, were imported. Therefore all Mastiffs in the late 1950s were descended from Nydia and the 14 Mastiffs previously mentioned. It has been alleged that the Mastiff was bred with other more numerous giant breeds such as Bullmastiffs and St. Bernards, as these were considered close relatives to the Mastiff. In 1959, a Dogue de Bordeaux, Fidelle de Fenelon, was imported from France to the USA, registered as a Mastiff, and entered the gene pool. Since that time, the breed has gradually been restored in Britain, has reached 28th most popular breed in the USA , and is now found worldwide.

Miscellaneous

Extract from Abraham Fleming's translation of John Caius's description, dated 1570, of the "Mastiue or Bandogge".

"This kinde of Dogge called a Mastyue or Bandogge is vaste, huge, stubborne, ougly, and eager, of a heuy and burthenous body, and therefore but of litle swiftnesse, terrible, and frightfull to beholde, and more fearce and fell then any Arcadian curre (notwithstãding they are sayd to hane their generation of the violent Lyon.) They are called Villatici, because they are appoynted to watche and keepe farme places and coũtry cotages sequestred from commõ recourse, and not abutting vpon other houses by reason of distaunce, when there is any feare conceaued of theefes, robbers, spoylers, and night wanderers. They are seruiceable against the Foxe and the Badger, to drive wilde and tame swyne out of Medowes, pastures, glebelandes *(church lands)* and places planted with fruite, to bayte and take the bull by the eare, when occasion so requireth. One dogge or two at the vttermost, sufficient for that purpose be the bull neuer so monsterous, neuer so fearce, neuer so furious, neuer so stearne, neuer so vntameable. For it is a kinde of dogge capeable of courage, violent and valiaunt, striking could feare into the harts of men, but standing in feare of no man, in so much that no weapons will make him shrincke, nor abridge his boldnes. Our Englishe men (to th' intent that theyr dogges might be the more fell and fearce) assist nature with arte, vse, and custome, for they teach theyr dogges to baite the Beare, to baite the Bull and other such like cruell and bloudy beastes (appointing an ouerseer of the game) without any collar to defend theyr throtes, and oftentimes they traine them vp in fighting and wrestling with a man hauing for the safegarde of his lyfe, eyther a Pikestaffe, a clubbe, or a sworde and by vsing them to such exercises as these, theyr dogges become more sturdy and strong. The force which is in them surmounteth all beleefe, the fast holde which they take with their teeth exceedeth all credit, three of them against a Beare, fowre against a Lyon are sufficient, both to try masteryes with them and vtterly to ouermatch them."

Extract from Barnaby Googe's translation of Conrad Heresbach's description dated 1631 of the Bandog for the house:

"First, the Mastie that keepeth the house. For this purpose you must provide you such a one as hath a large and mightie body, a great shrill voyce, that both with his barking he may discover, and with his sight dismaye the theefe, yea, being not seene, with the horror of his voice put him to flight. His stature must be neither long nor short, but well set ; his head, great ; his eyes, sharp and fiery, either browne or grey ; his lippes, blackish, neither turning up nor hanging too much down ; his mouth black and wide ; his neather jaw, fat, and coming out of it on either side a fang appearing more outward than his other teeth ; his upper teeth even with his neather, not hanging too much over, sharpe, and hidden with his lippes ; his countenance, like a lion ; his brest, great and shag hayrd ; his shoulders, broad ; his legges, bigge ; his tayle, short ; his feet, very great. His disposition must neither be too gentle nor too curst, that he neither faune upon a theefe nor flee upon his friends; very waking; no gadder abroad, nor lavish of his mouth, barking without cause; neither maketh it any matter though he be not swifte, for he is but to fight at home, and to give warning of the enemie."

Sydenham Edwards (1800), wrote in the *Cynographia Britannica*, London: C. Whittingham:

"What the Lion is to the Cat the Mastiff is to the Dog, the noblest of the family; he stands alone, and all others sinking before him. His courage does not exceed its temper and generosity and in attachment he equals the kindest of his race. His docility is perfect; the teasing of the smaller kinds will hardly provoke him to resent, and I have seen him down with his paw the Terrier or cur that has bit him, without offering further injury. In a family he will permit the children to play with him and will suffer all their little pranks without offence. The blind ferocity of the bulldog will often wound the hand of the master who assists him to combat, but the Mastiff distinguishes perfectly, enters the field with temper, and engages the attack as if confident of success: if he overpowers, or is beaten, his master may take him immediately in his arms and fear nothing. This ancient and faithful domestic, the pride of our island, uniting the useful, the brave and the docile, though sought by foreign nations and perpetuated on the continent, is nearly extinct where he was probably an aborigine, or is bastardized by numberless crosses, everyone of which degenerate from the invaluable character of the parent, who was deemed worthy to enter the Roman amphitheatre and in the presence of the masters of the world, encounter the pard and assail even the lord of the savage tribes, whose courage was sublimed by torrid suns, and found none gallant enough to oppose him on the deserts of Zaara or the plains of Numidia."

Famous English Mastiffs

- "Zorba", at the largest dog as recorded by The Guiness Book of World Records
- "Crown Prince", progenitor of the modern breed, owned by psychiatrist L. Forbes Winslow
- "Cash", owned by Trevor Dwyer-Lynch ("Patrick" from Coronation Street), also appeared in one episode of the show
- "Hercules" (a.k.a. "the Beast"), from the film The Sandlot (played by Ch. Mtn. Oaks Gunner)
- "Goliath" (a.k.a. "the Great Fear"), from the film The Sandlot 2
- "Carlo" from The Adventure of the Copper Beeches, a Sherlock Holmes story
- "Zeus", owned by Mark Calaway (The Undertaker)
- "Bluto", owned by Paul Levesque (Triple H) and Stephanie McMahon
- "Kazak", owned by Winston Niles Rumfoord, a wealthy space traveler in Kurt Vonnegut's novel The Sirens of Titan
- "Moss" and "Jaguar", of the Japanese series Ginga: Nagareboshi Gin and its sequel Ginga Densetsu Weed
- "Mason The Mastiff" [1], in the 2007 film Transformers

- "Leo", owned by Richard Ansdell, R.A., and the model for his painting "The Poacher", aka "The Poacher At Bay"
- "Rocky" (Ch Sterling's Against All Odds) appeared in the "Leech Trapper" episode of the TV series Dirty Jobs
- "Lady Marton", owned by Victorian industrialist Henry Bolckow, and claimed by some to have been a St. Bernard

Clubs by country

Country	Club Name
Australia	Mastiff Club Of Victoria Inc. [2]
Austria	Molosser Club Austria [3]
Belgium	Mastiff Club Belgium [4]
Canada	Canadian Mastiff Club [5]
Canada	Mastiff Fanciers of Western Canada [6]
Czech Republic	Moloss Club CZ [7]
Denmark	Dansk Mastiff Klub [8]
France	Club français du Bullmastiff et du Mastiff [9]
Germany	Old English Mastiff Club Deutschland e.V. [10]
New Zealand	New Zealand Mastiff Club [11]
Norway	Norwegian English Mastiff Club [12]
Spain	Club Espanol de los Molosos de Arena [13]
Sweden	Svenska Mastiffklubben [14]
United Kingdom	Old English Mastiff Club [15]
United Kingdom	Mastiff Association [16]
United States	Garden State Mastiff Fanciers [17]
United States	Mastiff Club of America [18]
United States	Mid-west Mastiff Fanciers [19]

United States	Pacific Northwest Mastiff Fanciers [20]
United States	Pacific Southwest Mastiff Club [21]
United States	Lone Star Mastiff Fanciers [22]
United States	Redwood Empire Mastiff Club [23]

See also

- Molosser
- Molossus
- Alaunt
- Pugnaces Britanniae
- Bandog
- Alpine Mastiff
- Bullmastiff
- Spanish Mastiff
- Pyrenean Mastiff
- Neapolitan Mastiff
- Tibetan Mastiff
- Dogue de Bordeaux (French Mastiff)
- Broholmer (Danish Mastiff)
- German Mastiff (Great Dane)
- Boerboel (South African Mastiff)
- Fila Brasileiro
- Alangu Mastiff (Indian Mastiff)
- Bully Kutta (Pakistani Mastiff, Sindh Mastiff)
- Tibetan Mastiff
- Cane Corso
- Japanese Mastiff
- Caucasian Shepherd Dog
- Central Asian Ovcharka
- American Mastiff
- Korean Mastiff
- Pug a dog of the Toy Group considered by some to be a miniature breed of mastiff, originating in China.

References

- http://www.guinnessworldrecords.com/records/natural_world/fantastic_pets/tallest_dog_living.aspx
- http://www.snopes.com/photos/animals/hercules.asp#photo

External links

- Mastiffs in Need or Distress Rescue [1]
- Great Lakes Mastiff Rescue [2]
- Mastiff Association [16]
- Molosser World [3]
- Mastiff Secrets: The Ultimate Guide [4]
- http://www.snopes.com/photos/animals/hercules.asp#photo
- http://www.guinnessworldrecords.com/records/natural_world/fantastic_pets/tallest_dog_living.aspx

Neapolitan Mastiff

The **Neapolitan Mastiff**, **Italian Mastiff**, (**Mastino Napoletano** in italian) is a large, ancient dog breed. This massive breed is often used as a guard and defender of family and property due to their protective instincts and their fearsome appearance. The breed is reported to have been used to fight alongside the Roman Legions, by having bladed and spiked leather harnesses tied to their backs and being trained to run under the bellies of enemy horses, to disembowel them.

Size and proportion

According to the American Kennel Club (AKC) standards , male Neapolitan Mastiffs should measure 26–31 inches (66–79 cm) at the withers, weighing 170 pounds (70 kg), but can easily reach up to 200 pounds (90 kg) for larger males, while females should be 24–29 inches (61–74 cm) and weigh around 140 pounds (64 kg). Body length should be 10-15% more than that of the height.

Temperament

The Neapolitan Mastiff is fearless and extremely protective of its home and family. They prefer to be with their family and to remain in and around the home at all times. The Neapolitan Mastiff rarely barks unless under provocation, renowned for sneaking up on intruders as opposed to first alerting them of their presence.

Neos, as a breed, are extremely intelligent dogs with a tendency to be independent thinkers. They learn quickly, which is both good *and* bad, since this guardian breed needs extensive proper socialization to learn to accept strangers, especially within the home; without proper early socialization and training, these dogs are likely to become aggressive towards strangers and unfamiliar dogs. Like with other breeds, forceful training methods, "alpha roles", and a general "dominance" mentality will not work with these dogs, especially since it is difficult to try to physically dominate a dog that is as large as an adult; if you want a well mannered dog, prevent problems before they happen by using positive training methods, beginning socializing early, and continuing socializing throughout life.

The Neapolitan Mastiff is not a breed for most people, and certainly not a dog for beginners. As a general rule, Neapolitan Mastiffs are not appropriate for homes with small children, as Neos are large, powerful dogs and don't always know their own strength. Additionally, young children have young friends, and even with extensive socialization and training, Neapolitans will be wary of strangers and protective of their family, which can be disastrous for small children.

Additional protection training is unnecessary because they are natural guard dogs and always have been. As with every breed, obedience training is very important. The Mastino is very tolerant of pain due to the breed's early fighting background and the fact the skin is loose on the body, so it is important to routinely check for health problems, as a Neo may not behave differently when injured or ill. They also are renowned for drooling especially after drinking or if they get excited. Their temperament and protective instincts are noticeably sharper as compared to allied "heavy molosser" breeds such as the Dogue de Bordeaux, the English Mastiff, the Mastín Español etc. and therefore they have been used as a breed component in the development of many modern protection breeds such as the Swinford Bandog (also known as the American Bandog Mastiff) and others. This breed is not particularly dog-aggressive, but males are known to be very dominant and, at times, confrontational.

Health

The Neo is generally hardy, but like all breeds, has some specific health concerns. The most common is Cherry eye. Others include:

- Hip dysplasia
- Ectropion
- Entropion
- Elbow dysplasia
- Progressive retinal atrophy
- Hypothyroidism
- Cardiomyopathy
- Bloat
- Skin infections between skin folds called Pyoderma
- Anesthetic Sensitivity

Additionally, Neos do not do well in hot weather, and are prone to heatstroke. Like most giant breeds, the Neapolitan Mastiff is not particularly long-lived, averaging 7 to 9 years, however, with a proper biologically appropriate diet, safe exercise, and proper weight maintenance, there is no reason that the average Neo cannot live beyond that.

Care and maintenance

When it comes to exercise, Neapolitans are not a very active breed as their energy tends to be short lived and their weight causes stress to their joints when excessive. However, they can and will have short, extremely powerful bursts of energy.

History

The Neapolitan Mastiff is one of the Molosser type of dogs, which probably descend from a common stock; whether this was the Molossus attested in antiquity is controversial.

Despite centuries of popularity throughout Europe, this type of dog was almost lost after World War II. Soon after the war, Italian painter Piero Scanziani established a breeding kennel to turn the mastiff-type dogs of Italy into a formal breed which was then named the Neapolitan Mastiff and English Mastiff was used to help in this process.

Neapolitan Mastiffs in the media

- Alan from the film *Babe: Pig in the City.*
- Fang from the Harry Potter films (in the books, Fang is a boarhound, an old term for a Great Dane, while in the films he is a Neapolitan Mastiff).
- Pansy [1] from the Burke series of novels by Andrew Vachss.
- Sweetie from Robert K. Tanenbaum's *Butch Karp* novels.
- A Neapolitan was recently featured in the movie American Gangster as a domestic pet belonging to an Italian Mafia Boss.
- A Neapolitan Mastiff appears in a scene in the movie *DragonHeart.*
- Used in the movie air buddies as the police dog named sniffer.

External links

- Neapolitan Mastiff Rescue [2]
- Neapolitan Mastiff Welfare UK [3]

Newfoundland (dog)

The **Newfoundland** is a large breed of dog. Newfoundlands can be black, brown, grey, or black and white (Landseer). They were originally bred and used as a working dog for fishermen in Newfoundland, Canada. They are famously known for their giant size and tremendous strength, sweet dispositions, and loyalty. Newfoundland dogs excel at water rescue, due to their great muscles and their webbed feet and acute swimming abilities. Newfoundland dogs require daily (possibly every 2 days) brushing with a hard brush. Newfoundland puppies are laid-back and considered easy to housebreak. The breed is thought to be the strongest of any dog breed—even beating some characteristics of the Great Dane, Mastiff, or Irish Wolfhound.

Description

Appearance

Newfoundlands ('Newfs', 'Newfies') have webbed feet and a water-resistant coat. Males weigh 60–70 kg (130-150 lb), and females 45–55 kg (100-120 lb), placing them in the "Giant" weight range. Some Newfoundland dogs have been known to weigh over 90 kg (200 lb). The largest Newfoundland on record weighed 120 kg (260 lbs) and measured over 6 feet from nose to tail, ranking it among the biggest Molossers. They may grow up to 22-28 inches tall at the shoulder.

The American Kennel Club (AKC) standard colors of the Newfoundland dogs are black, brown, gray, and landseer (black or brown head and white and black body); The Kennel Club (KC) permits only black, brown, and landseer; the Canadian Kennel Club (CKC) permanents are only black and landseer. The **Landseer** is named after the artist Sir Edwin Henry Landseer, who featured them in many of his paintings. AKC, CKC, and KC all treat Landseer as part of the breed. Fédération Cynologique Internationale (FCI) consider the Landseer to be a separate breed; others consider it only a Newfoundland color variation.

The Newfoundland's extremely large bones give him mass, while his mammoth musculature gives him the power he needs to take on rough ocean waves and powerful tides. He has an enormous lung capacity for swimming extremely long distances, and a thick, oily and waterproof double coat which protects him from the chill of icy waters. His droopy lips and jowls make the dog drool, but the purpose of his design gives passageways that allow him to breathe even when his mouth is full and swamped by waves.

In the water, his massive webbed paws gives the Newfoundland another advantage, giving him maximum propulsion with every stroke. The stroke is not an ordinary dog paddle. Unlike other dogs, the Newfoundland moves his limbs in a down-and-out motion, which can be seen as a modified breaststroke. This gives him more power with every stroke.

Temperament

"Sweetness of temperament is the hallmark of the Newfoundland; this is the most important single characteristic of the breed." - Newfoundland Club Of America.

"Its soft expression reflects its benevolent and dignified temperament." - Animal Planet about the great Newfoundland Dog.

The Newfoundland dog is legendarily known for its benevolence and its strength. It is known to be one of the kindest and gentlest dogs. It is for this reason that this breed is known as "the gentle giant". International kennel clubs generally describe the breed as having a sweet temper. It has a deep loud bark, is easy to train, makes a fine guardian or watchdog, and is extremely good with children.

The Newfoundland dog is also extremely good with other animals. Its caring and gentle nature comes out in play and interaction with humans and animals alike. As with any breed, the Newfoundland can have dominance issues, but this is unusual for the breed.

Health

There are several health problems associated with Newfoundlands. Newfoundlands are prone to hip dysplasia (a malformed ball and socket in the hip joint). They also get Elbow dysplasia, and cystinuria (a hereditary defect that forms calculi stones in the bladder). Another genetic problem is subvalvular aortic stenosis. This is a common heart defect in Newfoundlands involving defective heart valves. SAS can cause sudden death at an early age.

History

The Newfoundland shares many unmistakable characteristics with the St. Bernard and English mastiff, including a short, stout legs, massive heads with very broad snouts, a thick bull neck, and a very sturdy bone structure. These features are likely the result of a shared ancestry from the Alpine mastiff. The breed originated in Newfoundland and is descended from a breed indigenous to the island that later became known as the St. John's Dog. The speculation they may be partly descended from the big black bear dogs introduced by the Vikings in 1001 A.D. is based more in romance than in fact. The modern day Newfoundland is not the descendant of St. Bernards but the other way around: Newfoundlands were brought and introduced to St. Bernards was because of an epidemic of distemper in St. Bernards. By the time colonization was permitted in 1610, the distinct physical characteristics and mental attributes had been established in the breed. In the early 1880s fishermen and explorers from Ireland and England traveled to the Grand Banks of Newfoundland, where they described two main types of working dog. One was heavily built, large with a longish coat, and the other medium-sized in build - an active, smooth-coated water dog. The heavier breed was known as the Greater Newfoundland, or Newfoundland. The smaller breed was known as the Lesser Newfoundland, or St. John's Dog - the founding breed of the modern Labrador Retriever. Both breeds were used as working dogs to pull fish nets, with the Greater Newfoundland also being used to haul carts, and other equipment.

Many tales have been told of the courage displayed by Newfoundlands in adventuring and lifesaving exploits. Over the last two centuries, this has inspired a number of artists, who have portrayed the dogs in paint, stone, bronze and porcelain. One famous Newfoundland was a dog named Seaman, who accompanied American explorers Lewis and Clark on their expedition.

The breed prospered in the United Kingdom, until 1914 and again in 1939, when its numbers were almost fatally depleted by wartime restrictions. Since the 1950s there has been a steady increase in numbers and popularity, despite the fact that the Newfoundland's great size, appetite, and fondness for mud and water makes it unsuitable as a pet for most households.

Rescues

During the Discovery Channel's second day of coverage of the AKC Eukanuba National Championship on December 3, 2006, anchor Bob Goen reported that Newfoundlands exhibit a very strong propensity to rescue people from water. Goen stated that one Newfoundland alone once aided the rescue of 63 shipwrecked sailors. Today, kennel clubs across the United States host Newfoundland Rescue Demonstrations, as well as offering classes in the field.

An unnamed Newfoundland is credited for saving Napoleon Bonaparte in 1815. During his famous escape from exile on the island of Elba, rough seas knocked Napoleon overboard. A fisherman's dog jumped into the sea, and kept Napoleon afloat until he could reach safety.

In 1832, Ann Harvey of Isle aux Morts, her father, and a Newfoundland Dog named Hairyman saved over 180 Irish immigrants from the wreck of the brig Dispatch.

In the early 1900s, a dog that is thought to have been a Newfoundland saved 92 people who were on a sinking ship in Newfoundland during a blizzard. The dog retrieved a rope thrown out into the turbulent waters by those on deck, and brought the rope to shore to people waiting on the beach. A breeches buoy was attached to the rope, and all those aboard the ship were able to get across to the shore.

In 1995, a 10-month old Newfoundland named Boo saved a deaf-mute from drowning in the Yuba River in Northern California. The man fell into the river while dredging for gold. Boo noticed the struggling man as he and his owner were walking along the river. The Newfoundland instinctively knew to dive into the river, take the drowning man by the arm, and bring him to safety. According to Janice Anderson, the Newfoundland's breeder, Boo had received no formal training in water rescue.

Further evidence of Newfoundlands' ability to rescue or support life saving activities was cited in a recent article by the BBC.

Quotations

"The man they had got now was a jolly, light-hearted, thick-headed sort of a chap, with about as much sensitiveness in him as there might be in a Newfoundland puppy. You might look daggers at him for an hour and he would not notice it, and it would not trouble him if he did." Jerome K. Jerome *Three Men in a Boat*

"Newfoundland dogs are good to save children from drowning, but you must have a pond of water handy and a child, or else there will be no profit in boarding a Newfoundland." Josh Billings

"A man is not a good man to me because he will feed me if I should be starving, or warm me if I should be freezing, or pull me out of a ditch if I should ever fall into one. I can find you a Newfoundland dog that will do as much." Henry David Thoreau *Walden*

"Near this spot are deposited the remains of one who possessed Beauty without Vanity, Strength without Insolence, Courage without Ferocity, and all the Virtues of Man, without his Vices. This Praise, which would be unmeaning Flattery if inscribed over human ashes, is but a just tribute to the Memory of Boatswain, a Dog." George Gordon, Lord Byron, Epitaph to a Dog.

"That boat, Rover by name, which, though now in strange seas, had often pressed the beach of Captain Delano's home, and, brought to its threshold for repairs, had familiarly lain there, as a Newfoundland dog; the sight of that household boat evoked a thousand trustful associations..." Herman Melville *Benito Cereno*

"Your fatuous specialist is now beginning to rebuke "secondrate" newspapers for using such phrases as "to suddenly go" and "to boldly say". I ask you, Sir, to put this man out without interfering with his perfect freedom of choice between "to suddenly go", to go suddenly" and "suddenly to go". Set him adrift and try an intelligent Newfoundland dog in his place." George Bernard Shaw, letter to the Chronicle newspaper (1892)

Famous Newfoundlands

- **Adam** - **Seaward's Blackbeard** - 1984 Best in Show winner at the Westminster Dog Show
- **Boatswain** - pet of English poet Lord Byron and the subject of his poem Epitaph to a Dog
- **Bilbo** - lifeguard at sennon cove beach in Cornwall
- **Brumus** - Robert F. Kennedy's dog
- **Brutus** - first dog to complete the Appalachian Mountain Club's "Winter 48", climbing all 48 peaks in one calendar winter
- **Carlo** - Emily Dickinson's dog
- **Faithful** - First dog of President Ulysses S. Grant
- **Frank** - Unofficial mascot of the Orphan Brigade during the American Civil War
- **Gander** the Mascot of the Royal Rifles of Canada who was killed in action at the Battle of Hong Kong when he carried a grenade away from wounded soldiers. For this he was awarded the PDSA

Dickin Medal retroactively in 2000.

- **Hairy Man** - The dog who helped Ann Harvey and her father and brother rescue 163 people from a shipwreck.
- **Hector** - First dog of President Rutherford B. Hayes
- **Josh** - **Darbydale's All Rise Pouchcove** - 2004 Best in Show winner at the Westminster Dog Show
- **Lara** - First dog of President James Buchanan
- **Pluto** - pet of the Croatian operatic soprano Ilma de Murska, which used to dine at table with her and was trained to eat a cooked fowl from a place setting without dripping gravy on the tablecloth. Pluto lived in the 1860s.
- **Porthos** - pet of J. M. Barrie Inspiration for "Nana", pet of the Darling family in Peter Pan.
- **Robber** - dog of Richard Wagner who accompanied him on his flight from his creditors from Riga on a fishing boat, which inspired the opera *The Flying Dutchman.*
- **Russ** - last dog of Richard Wagner, buried at the feet of his master in the composer's tomb in the park of Villa Wahnfried in Bayreuth, under his own plaque: "Here rests and watches Wagner's Russ."
- **Sable Chief** - mascot of Royal Newfoundland Regiment
- **Swansea Jack** - Famous Welsh rescue dog
- **Seaman** - companion of explorer Meriwether Lewis
- **Jack** - national champion and gold medalist, resident of Cary, North Carolina

Famous fictional Newfoundlands

- **Crusoe** - main character of *The Dog Crusoe*, by R.M. Ballantine.
- **Jakob** - hero and one of the main characters in the 1977 Slovenian movie *Sreca na vrvici*
- **Lou** - companion to Officers Mahoney and Shtulman in the 1985 movie *Police Academy 2*
- **Mother Teresa** - major canine character in the movie *Must Love Dogs*
- **Murphy** - main canine character in Kevin Fritz children's book *The Newf and The Dane* (2003)
- **Pilot** - pet of Edward Fairfax Rochester in Charlotte Brontë's classic novel *Jane Eyre* (1847) - first described in chapter 12
- **Sirius** - dog of Maggie in the Joan Hiatt Harlow juvenile fiction book *Star in the Storm*
- **Skipper** - Billy Topsail's dog in Norman Duncan's*The Adventures of Billy Topsail* (1906)
- **Thunder** - from the children's book *Thunder from the Sea* by Joan Hiatt Harlow and Wendell Minor
- **Jim (Effrijim)** - a demon in the form of a Newfoundland dog from the Katie MacAlister book *You Slay Me* (Aisling Grey Series)
- **Nana** - from "Peter Pan"

External links

- The Newfoundland Dog Club Of Canada [1]
- Newfoundland Club of America [2]
- The Newfoundland Club (UK) [3]
- The Newfoundland Club of Ireland [4]
- Newfoundland Club Inc. of New Zealand [5]
- Newfoundland Health Information [6]

Portuguese Water Dog

The **Portuguese Water Dog** is a breed of working dog as classified by the American Kennel Club. Portuguese Water Dogs are originally from the Portuguese region of the Algarve, from where the breed expanded to all around Portugal's coast, where they were taught to herd fish into fishermen's nets, to retrieve lost tackle or broken nets, and to act as couriers from ship to ship, or ship to shore. Portuguese Water Dogs rode in bobbing fishing trawlers as they worked their way from the warm Atlantic waters of Portugal to the frigid fishing waters off the coast of Iceland where the fleets caught cod to bring home. Portuguese Water Dogs were often taken with sailors during the Portuguese discoveries.

In Portugal, the breed is called **Cão de Água** (pronounced *Kow-dee-Ah-gwa*; literally "water dog"). In its native land, the dog is also known as the Algarvian Water Dog ("Cão de Água Algarvio"), or Portuguese Fishing Dog (*Cão Pescador Português*). *Cão de Água de Pêlo Ondulado* is the name given the wavy-haired variety, and *Cão de Água de Pêlo Encaracolado* is the name for the curly-coated variety.

The Portuguese Water Dog is a fairly rare breed; only 15 entrants for Portuguese Water Dogs were made to England's Crufts competition in 2002. Though some breeders claim they are a hypoallergenic dog breed, there is no scientific evidence to support the claim that hypoallergenic dog breeds exist. However, their non-shedding qualities have made them more popular in recent years.

Description

The closest relatives of the PWD are widely thought to be the Barbet and Standard Poodle. Like Poodles and several other water dog breeds, PWDs are highly intelligent, can have curly coats, have webbed toes for swimming, and do not shed. However, Portuguese Water Dogs are more robustly built, with stout legs, and can have a wavy coat instead of tightly curled. If comparing the structure to that of a Poodle, there are significant differences between the two breeds. The Portuguese Water Dog built of strong substantial bone; well developed, neither refined nor coarse, and a solidly built, muscular body. The Portuguese Water Dog is off-square, slightly longer than tall when measured from prosternum to rearmost point of the buttocks, and from withers to ground. Portuguese Water Dog eyes are black or various tones of brown, and their coats can be black, brown, black and white or brown and white.

Male Portuguese Water Dogs usually grow to be about 20 to 23 inches (51 cm to 58 cm) tall, and they weigh between 40 and 60 pounds (18 kg to 27 kg), while the females usually grow to be about 17 to 21 inches (43 cm to 53 cm) tall, and they weigh between 35 and 50 pounds.

PWDs have a single-layered coat that does not shed (see Moult), and therefore their presence is tolerated extremely well among many people who suffer from dog allergies. Some call PWDs hypoallergenic dogs, but any person with dog allergies who would like a dog with these qualities should actually spend time with the animals before purchasing, to test whether the dog is truly non-allergenic to them.

Most PWDs, especially those shown in conformation shows, are entirely black, black and white, brown, or silver-tipped; it is common to see white chest spots and white paws or legs on black or brown coated dogs. "Parti" or "Irish-marked" coats, with irregular white and black spots, are rare but visually striking. "Parti" dogs are becoming more common in the United States. However, in Portugal the breed standard does not allow more than 30% white markings. Overall, white is the least common Portuguese Water Dog color, while black with white markings on the chin ("milk chin") and chest is the most common color combination.

Coat types

This breed does not shed its hair. The hair is either wavy or curly. Many dogs have mixed pattern hair: curly all over the body but wavy on the tail and ears.

From the Portuguese Water Dog Club of America Revised Standard for the Portuguese Water Dog come these descriptions of the two coat types:

- Curly coat: "Compact, cylindrical curls, somewhat lusterless. The hair on the ears is sometimes wavy."
- Wavy coat: "Falling gently in waves, not curls, and with a slight sheen."

If left untended, the hair on a PWD will keep growing indefinitely. Problems associated with this include the hair around the eyes growing so long as to impede vision, and matting of the body hair, which can cause skin irritations. For these reasons, PWDs must be trimmed about every two months and the coat brushed every other day. This is not the breed for those humans wishing to have a low maintenance breed. In addition to the grooming, which typically costs between $75–100 a session, this breed requires daily exercise and consistently firm yet positive training techniques. Although it is possible to groom them at home, many owners find it easier to pay a professional groomer and, to avoid matting, they brush out the coat regularly between groomings.

Improper coat

Occasionally, a dog may have what is termed an "improper" coat. This genetic condition causes the dog to have an undercoat. Because improperly coated PWDs do not adhere to the breed standard, they may not be shown in conformation competition. Otherwise they are completely healthy and have all the excellent traits of the breed. They should not be used in breeding programs, because improper coat is an inherited condition.

Grooming styles

The hair of PWDs grows continually and requires regular brushing and cutting or clipping. The coat is usually worn in a "retriever cut" or a "lion cut".

The lion cut

In the lion cut, the hindquarters, muzzle, and the base of the tail are shaved and the rest of the body is left full length. This cut originated with the fishing dogs of Portugal. This is the traditional cut and perhaps the most functional, given the breed's main historical significance as a fisherman's companion. The lion cut diminished the initial impact and shock of cold water when the breed jumped from the boats, as well as providing warmth to the vitals. The hindquarters were left shaved to allow easier movement of the back legs and the breed's powerful, rudder-like tail.

The retriever cut

The retriever cut is left 1" (2.5 cm) long evenly over the body (although some owners prefer the muzzle or the base of the tail shorter). This cut is a more recent style and originated because breeders wanted to make the breed more appealing and less unusual looking for buyers.

Sometimes owners will clip the hair of their dogs very short, especially in the summer months, in modified retriever cut.

Vocalisation

Portuguese Water Dogs have a multi-octave voice. They tend to be quiet dogs although they will warn when the home is approached, and they will communicate their desires vocally and behaviourally to their owner. Their bark is loud and distinctive. They may engage in "expressive panting", by making a distinct "ha-ha-ha-ha" sound as an invitation to play or to indicate a desire for nearby food. They sometimes whine.

The PWD's biddability, high intelligence, and tendency to vocalise and then seek out its human master when specific alarms occur make it an ideal hearing-ear or deaf-assistance dog. PWDs can be readily trained to bark loudly when a telephone rings, and then to find and alert a hard-of-hearing or deaf master.

Temperament

Portuguese Water dogs make excellent companions. They are loving, independent, and intelligent and are easily trained in obedience and agility skills. Once introduced, they are generally friendly to strangers, and enjoy being petted, which, due to their soft, fluffy coats, is a favour that human beings willingly grant them.

Because they are working dogs, PWDs are generally content in being at their master's side, awaiting directions, and, if they are trained, they are willing and able to follow complex commands. They learn very quickly, seem to enjoy the training, and have a long memory for the names of objects. These traits and their non-shedding coats mean they excel at the various Service Dog roles such as hearing dogs (assistance dogs for the deaf), mobility dogs, and seizure response dogs. They also make unusually good therapy dogs.

A PWD usually stays in proximity to its owners, indoors as well as outdoors. This is typical of the breed. Though very gregarious animals, these dogs will typically bond with one primary or alpha family member. Some speculate that this intense bonding arose in the breed because the dogs were selected to work in proximity to their masters on small fishing boats, unlike other working dogs such as herding dogs and water dogs that range out to perform tasks. In any case, the modern PWD, whether employed on a boat or kept as a pet or a working dog, loves water, attention, and prefers to be engaged in activity within sight of a human partner. This is not a breed to be left alone for long periods of time, indoors or out.

As water dogs, the PWD's retrieving instinct is strong, which also gives some dogs tugging and chewing tendencies.

A PWD will commonly jump as a greeting. Owners may choose to limit this behavior. Some PWDs may walk, hop, or "dance" on their hind legs when greeting or otherwise enthusiastic. Some PWDs will stand upright at kitchen counters and tables, especially if they smell food above them. This habit is known as "counter surfing" and is characteristic of the breed. Although it can be a nuisance, many PWD owners evidently enjoy seeing their dogs walking, hopping, standing up, or "countering" and do not seriously discourage these activities.

While they are very good companions to people who understand what they need, Portuguese Water Dogs are not for everyone. Because of their intelligence and working drive, they require regular intensive exercise as well as mental challenges. They are gentle and patient — but not "couch potatoes", and boredom may cause them to become destructive.

History

In ancient times

One theory is that some of the rugged Asian herding dogs were captured by the Berbers, a people who spread slowly across the face of North Africa to Morocco. Their descendants, the Moors, arrived in Portugal in the 8th century, bringing the water dogs with them.

Another theory purports that some of the dogs left the Asian steppes with the Goths, a confederation of German tribes. Some, (the Ostrogoths), went west and their dogs became the German poodle, called in German the poodle-hund or puddle-dog, that is, water-dog. Others, (the Visigoths), went south to fight the Romans, and their dogs became the Lion Dog, groomed in the traditional lion cut. In 400 CE, the Visigoths invaded Iberia (modern Spain and Portugal, then known as Hispania) and the dogs found their homeland.

A Portuguese Water Dog is first described in 1297 in a monk's account of a drowning sailor who was pulled from the sea by a dog with a "black coat, the hair long and rough, cut to the first rib and with a tail tuft".

"History of the Portuguese Water Dog", Kathryn Braund and Deyanne Farrell Miller, *The Complete Portuguese Water Dog*, 1986, webpage: DeLeao [1].

These theories explain how the Poodle and the Portuguese Water Dog may have developed from the same ancient genetic pool. At one time the Poodle was a longer-coated dog, as is one variety of the Portuguese Water Dog. The possibility also exists that some of the long-coated water dogs grew up with the ancient Iberians. In early times, Celtiberians migrated from lands which now belong to southwestern Germany. Swarming over the Pyrenees, circulating over the whole of western Europe, they established bases in Iberia, as well as in Ireland, Wales, and Brittany. The Irish Water Spaniel and Kerry Blue Terrier are believed by some to be descendants of the Portuguese Water Dog.

Modern day

The PWD was a breed on the verge of extinction when, during the 1930s, Vasco Bensaude, a wealthy Portuguese shipping magnate, began to seek out fishermen's dogs and utilize them in a breeding program to re-establish the breed. Bensaude's kennel was named Algarbiorum, and his most famous dog was Leão (1931–1942), a very "type-y" fisherman's stud dog who was bred to so many different females that about half of the pedigreed Portuguese Water Dogs in existence can trace their lineage back to him. Bensaude was aided by two Portuguese veterinarians, Dr. Francisco Pinto Soares and Dr. Manuel Fernandes Marques. His work was carried on by Conchita Cintron de Castelo Branco, to whom he gave his last 17 PWDs and all his archives.

Dr. António Cabral was the founder of the Avalade kennels in Portugal. Ch. Charlie de Avalade (Charlie), a brown-coated dog, and C. B. Baluarte de Avalade (Balu) were two of his many famous

PWDs. He registered his first PWD in 1954, after Bensaude had pioneered the re-establishment of the breed in Portugal. Cabral worked with Carla Molinari, Deyanne Miller, Sonja Santos and others to establish PWDs in the US. The "Mark of Cabral" is a triangular shape of different color/textured hair, usually a few inches from the base of the tail. You can see it more easily on a fresh lion clip—it can look like the clipper got too close.

Deyanne Miller is the single person most responsible for the rise of the PWD in America. In 1972, the Millers, along with 14 other people, formed the Portuguese Water Dog Club of America, Inc. (PWDCA). She worked with dogs from both the Cintron and Cabral lineages to establish a stable genetic pool of PWDs in the United States at her Farmion kennels. Another early US breeder of PWDs was the actor Raymond Burr.

Genetic diseases

As with all purebred dogs, PWDs are vulnerable to certain genetic defects. Due to the limited gene pool for this breed, conscientious breeders carefully study pedigrees and select dogs to minimize the chance of genetic disease and improper coat. Unfortunately, like many breeds, a growing popularity has encouraged breeding by people who are not knowledgeable about the breed.

Hip dysplasia

Like poodles, PWDs are vulnerable to hip dysplasia. However, the risk of a PWD developing hip dysplasia can be greatly reduced by thoroughly checking the pedigrees and health clearances in both the sire and dam of your dog. Hip dysplasia is a congenital and developmental problem with the hip joints.

Cataracts, PRA, and distichiasis

Cataracts and PRA (Progressive Retinal Atrophy) are two eye diseases found in PWDs. As with hip dysplasia, some lines carry these defects more frequently than others. PRA, which causes "night blindness", may lead to complete blindness. Fortunately this is a simple recessive gene. DNA testing is now available which can identify a dog carrying the gene for PRA. Known as "Optigen Testing" a "normal" or "A" dog does not carry the gene for PRA. A "carrier" or "B" dog carries one copy of the PRA gene and the dog will NOT express the disease but may or may not pass the gene to offspring. An "affected" or "C" dog has two copies of the PRA version of the gene and will probably express the disease as late onset Progressive Retinal Atrophy. A "B" or "C" dog should be bred *only* to an "A" dog to ensure that any offspring will not express the disease.

Ingrown eyelashes (distichiasis) occurs in some curly-coated breeds, but is not particularly common in PWDs. Ingrown eyelashes will rub the eye causing extensive corneal ulcerations. The condition is minor so long as it is not ignored, and can be surgically treated if necessary.

GM1 Storage Disease

GM1 Storage Disease, one of a family of conditions called GM1 gangliosidoses, is a recessive, genetic disorder that is inevitably fatal. It is caused by a deficiency of beta-galactosidase, with resulting abnormal storage of acidic lipid materials in cells of the central and peripheral nervous systems, but particularly in the nerve cells. Because PWDs are all rather closely related to one another and share a limited gene pool, PWDs who were GM1 Storage Disease carriers were able to be genetically identified, and the condition has now been almost entirely eliminated from the breed. All breeding stock should be tested for GM-1 storage disease or GM1 gangliosidoses, which is a fatal nerve disease that typically appears when a puppy is approximately six months of age. The affected puppy will show clinical signs of cerebellar dysfunction including ataxia, tremors, paresis, and seizures. The pet may also exhibit a change in temperament. Lesions of the retina and clouding of the cornea may occur. GM-1 storage disease is a recessive deficiency of betagalactosidase. The condition has been genetically identified and is no longer common.

Juvenile Dilated Cardiomyopathy

Juvenile Dilated Cardiomyopathy is a rare, fatal condition caused by an autosomal recessive gene. It affects young dogs, who succumb to heart failure before reaching adulthood. As a simple recessive gene, it had been difficult to identify and was particularly heartbreaking as seemingly healthy puppies would suddenly die, often shortly after joining their adopted families. Since a recessive gene is responsible, that means if at least one parent is "normal" (that is, it does not carry a copy of the cardio version of the gene), its offspring can not contract the disease.

In 2007 a genetic linkage test became available which appears promising. This is not a test which confirms if a dog has, or doesn't have the disease; nor will it definitively predict the disease, as even if a dog is a JDC carrier this does not guarantee its offspring will suffer the disease. It only links certain strains of DNA as carriers of JDC. This is significant in that these strains can now largely be deselected for in the breeding process, as has been successful with GM1 Storage Disease (see above). The test is not yet complete for every bloodline, and *why* the identified strains are implicated is still unknown, and so in essence the *cause* of the condition remains a mystery to be solved.

Famous Portuguese Water Dogs

- U.S. Senator Ted Kennedy was the owner of three Portuguese Water Dogs: Splash, Sunny, and Cappy. Splash serves as the fictional narrator in Kennedy's children's book called *My Senator and Me: A Dog's-Eye View of Washington, D.C.*
- BARK team members feature Portuguese Water Dogs who retrieve home run balls that land in McCovey Cove, the body of water adjacent to AT&T Park. During every Sunday San Francisco Giants home game, these talented canines will work from boats and dive after splash hit baseballs that land in the water during batting practice and the game.
- It was revealed on April 11, 2009 that the First Puppy, the dog given to U.S. President Barack Obama's two daughters Sasha and Malia by Senator Ted Kennedy, was a Portuguese Water Dog. The girls have named the dog Bo because they have cousins with a cat of the same name and because Mrs. Obama's father was nicknamed Diddley, after the late musician Bo Diddley. The Obamas chose the breed because it is known to be less likely to stimulate allergic reactions.

References

- "Portuguese Water Dogs", Animal Planet, "Breed All About It" television series.

External links

- Seaworthy Portuguese Water Dogs [2]
- Portuguese Water Dog Club of Canada [3]
- The Portuguese Water Dog: Health Issues Concerning the Portuguese Water Dog [4]
- Portuguese Water Dog Club of Great Britain [5]
- Portuguese Water Dog Club of America [6]
- Portuguese Water Dog Foundation [7]
- The Norwegian Portuguese Water dog Club [8]
- PWD Stud Dogs and the PWD Pedigree Study Group [9]
- Portuguese Water Dog Information [10]
- Portuguese Water Dog FCI standard [11]
- Portuguese Water Dog Breed Profile [12]

Rottweiler

The **Rottweiler** is a medium to large size breed of domestic dog that originated in Rottweil, Germany. The dogs were known as "Rottweil butchers' dogs" () because they were used to herd livestock and pull carts laden with butchered meat and other products to market. Some records indicate that earlier Rottweilers may have also been used for hunting, although the modern Rottweiler has a relatively low hunting instinct. It is a hardy and very intelligent breed.

The Rottweiler was employed in its traditional roles until the mid-19th century when railroads replaced droving for getting livestock to market. While still used in herding, Rottweilers are now also used in search and rescue, as guide dogs for the blind, as guard or police dogs, and in other roles.

History

Although a versatile breed used in recent times for many purposes, the Rottweiler is primarily known as one of the oldest herding breeds. A multi-faceted herding and stock protection dog, it is capable of working all kinds of livestock under a variety of conditions.

The breed is ancient, one whose history stretches back to the Roman Empire. In those times, the Roman legion traveled with their meat on the hoof and required the assistance of working dogs to herd the cattle. One route the army traveled was through Württemberg and on to the small market town of Rottweil. The principal ancestors of the first Rottweilers during this time are believed to be the Roman droving dog, local dogs the army met on its travels, and dogs with molosser appearance coming from England and the Netherlands.

This region was eventually to become an important cattle area, and the descendants of the Roman cattle dogs proved their worth in both driving and protecting the cattle from robbers and wild animals. Rottweilers were said to have been used by travelling butchers at markets during the Middle Ages to guard money pouches tied around their necks. However, as railroads became the primary method for moving stock to market, the breed had declined so much that by 1900 there was only one female to be found in the town of Rottweil.

The build up to World War I saw a great demand for police dogs, and that led to a revival of interest in the Rottweiler. During the First and Second World Wars, Rottweilers were put into service in various roles, including as messenger, ambulance, draught, and guard dogs.

Deutscher Rottweiler-Klub (DRK, *German Rottweiler Club*), the first Rottweiler club in Germany, was founded 13 January 1907, and followed by the creation of the Süddeutscher Rottweiler-Klub (SDRK, *South German Rottweiler Club*) on 27 April 1907 and eventually became the IRK (International Rottweiler Club). The DRK counted around 500 Rottweilers, and the SDRK 3000 Rottweilers. The goals of the two clubs were different. The DRK aimed to produce working dogs and did not emphasize the morphology of the Rottweiler. The main stud dog of this club was Lord von der Teck. The IRK tried to produce a homogeneous morphology according to its standard. One of the main stud dogs of this club was Ralph von Neckar.

The various German Rottweiler Clubs amalgamated to form the Allgemeiner Deutscher Rottweiler Klub (ADRK, *General German Rottweiler Club*) in 1921. This was officially recorded in the register of clubs and associations at the district court of Stuttgart on 27 January 27 1924. The ADRK is recognised worldwide as the home club of the Rottweiler.

In 1935 the Rottweiler was officially recognized by the American Kennel Club. In 1936, Rottweilers were exhibited in Britain at Crufts. In 1966, a separate register was opened for the breed. In fact, in the mid 1990s, the popularity of the Rottweiler reached an all time high with it being the most registered dog by the American Kennel Club.

Technical description

"Rottweiler breeders aim at a dog of abundant strength, black coated with clearly defined rich tan markings, whose powerful appearance does not lack nobility and which is exceptionally well suited to being a companion, service and working dog."

1. Head (eyes)
2. Snout (teeth, tongue)
3. Dewlap (throat, neck skin)
4. Shoulder
5. Elbow
6. Forefeet
7. Highest Point of the Rump
8. Leg (thigh and hip)
9. Hock
10. Hind feet
11. Withers
12. Stifle
13. Paws
14. Tail

Head

The skull is of medium length, broad between the ears. The forehead line is moderately arched as seen from the side, with the occipital bone well developed without being conspicuous. The stop is well defined.

The Rottweiler nose is well developed, more broad than round, with relatively large nostrils and always black. The muzzle should appear neither elongated nor shortened in relation to the cranial region. The nasal bridge is broad at the base and moderately tapered.

The lips are black and close fitting with the corner of the mouth not visible. The gums should be as dark as possible.

Both the upper and lower jaws are strong and broad. According to the FCI Standard Rottweilers should have strong and complete dentition (42 teeth) with scissor bite, the upper incisors closely overlapping the lower incisors.

The zygomatic arches should be pronounced. The eyes should be of medium size, almond-shaped and dark brown in colour. The eyelids are close fitting.

The ears are medium-sized, pendant, triangular, wide apart, and set high on the head. With the ears laid forward close to the head, the skull appears to be broadened.

The skin on the head is tight fitting overall. When the dog is alert, the forehead may be slightly wrinkled.

Neck

The neck is strong, of fair length, well muscled, slightly arched, clean, free from throatiness, without dewlap and very long neck.

Body

The back is straight, strong and firm. The loins are short, strong and deep. The croup is broad, of medium length, and slightly rounded, neither flat nor falling away. The chest is roomy, broad and deep (approximately 50% of the shoulder height) with a well developed forechest and well sprung ribs. The flanks are not tucked up.

Tail

Natural bob tailed ("stumpy") or if present the tail was historically docked. Docking is banned in Germany, the U.K and some other countries. An un-docked Rottweiler tail is level in extension of the upper line; at ease it may be hanging.

Limbs

When seen from the front, the front legs are straight and not placed close to each other. The forearm, seen from the side, stands straight and vertical. The slope of the shoulder blade is about 45 degrees. The shoulders are well laid back. The upper arm is close fitting to the body. The forearm is strongly developed and muscular. Pasterns are slightly springy, strong but not steep. The front feet are round, tight and well arched, the pads hard, nails are short, black and strong.

When seen from behind, the rear legs are straight and not too close together. When standing free, obtuse angles are formed between the dog's upper thigh and the hip bone, the upper thigh and the lower thigh, and the lower thigh and metatarsal. The upper thigh is moderately long, broad and strongly muscled. The lower thigh is long, strongly and broadly muscled, sinewy. The hocks are sturdy, well angulated, not steep. The hind feet are slightly longer than the front feet. Toes are strong, arched, as tight as the front feet.

Gait

The Rottweiler is a trotting dog. In movement the back remains firm and relatively stable. Movement is harmonious, steady, full of energy and unrestricted, with good stride.

Coat

The coat consists of a top coat and an undercoat. The top coat is of medium length, coarse, dense and flat. The undercoat must not show through the top coat. The hair is a little longer on the hind-legs.

Rottweilers living in hot climates may have acclimatised and may be missing the undercoat.

Rottweiler coats tend to be low maintenance, although they experience heavy shedding prior to their seasons (females) or seasonally (males).

Size

Technically a "medium / large" breed, according to the FCI standard the Rottweiler stands 24-27 inches at the withers for males, 22-25 inches for females, and the average weight is 110-130 pounds(weight relative to height) for males and 90-105 pounds (weight is relative to height) for females.

Temperament

According to the FCI Standard, the Rottweiler is good-natured, placid in basic disposition, fond of children, very devoted, obedient, biddable and eager to work. Their appearance is natural and rustic, their behaviour self-assured, steady and fearless. They react to their surroundings with great alertness. The American Kennel Club says it is basically a calm, confident and courageous dog with a self-assured aloofness that does not lend itself to immediate and indiscriminate friendships. A Rottweiler is self-confident and responds quietly and with a wait-and-see attitude to influences in its environment. It has an inherent desire to protect home and family, and is an intelligent dog of extreme hardness and adaptability with a strong willingness to work, making them especially suited as a companion, guardian and general all-purpose dog.

Rottweilers are a powerful breed with well developed genetic herding and guarding instincts. As with any breed, potentially dangerous behavior in Rottweilers usually results from irresponsible ownership, abuse, neglect, or lack of socialization and training. However, the exceptional strength of the Rottweiler is an additional risk factor not to be neglected. It is for this reason that breed experts recommend that formal training and extensive socialization are essential for all Rottweilers. According to the AKC, Rottweilers love their people and may behave in a clownish manner toward family and friends, but they are also protective of their territory and do not welcome strangers until properly introduced. Obedience training and socialization are musts.

The breed has received some negative publicity. In the US, in a 1997 report by the CDC, the Rottweiler was listed as the second most likely breed of dog named in fatal human attacks, following Pit Bulls, although at approximately half the rate of the Pit Bull. Breed-specific bite rates are not known, and less responsible owners being drawn to certain breeds may be a factor. Dog related human fatalities need to be considered in the context that there are fewer than 30 dog related fatalities in the United States each year out of approximately 4.7 million bite incidents, from a total dog population estimated by the American Pet Products Association at 77.5 million dogs. A 2008 study surveying breed club members found that while Rottweilers were average in aggressiveness (bites or bite attempts) towards owners and other dogs, it indicated they tend to be more aggressive than average towards strangers. This aggression appears unrelated to the fear of the dog, but is correlated with watchdog and territorial instincts.

The portrayal of Rottweilers as evil dogs in several fictional films and TV series, most notably in *The Omen*, and negative press has added to their negative publicity. This has led to Rottweilers being banned in some municipalities and are sometimes targeted as dangerous dogs by legislation, such as in the Netherlands, Poland, Portugal and the Republic of Ireland. However, the Dutch law has since been changed as of 2008. On the other hand, not all mainstream media has portrayed the breed in a negative light: for example, a gentler side of the Rottweiler's personality was observed in the movie *Lethal Weapon 3* where a Rottweiler guarding a gun smuggling operation was placated by the main character, played by Mel Gibson, with dog treats. The dog was subsequently rescued and *de facto* adopted by the protagonist. Also, in the HBO series Entourage a Rottweiler named Arnold is a dear pet of the main characters. Cujo the loveable family dog and voice of the official website in the TV series *Kath and Kim*, is played by National Rottweiler Council (Australia) Champion and Dual Champion (Tracking) Goodiesway Basko (AI) CDX ET TSDX PT (pet name "Polo"). The hero of the picture book Good Dog, Carl! and its sequels is a Rottweiler, and quite favorably portrayed as a gentle, attentive, protective and intelligent guardian of his family members.

Working style

According to the American Kennel Club Rottweilers have a natural gathering style with a strong desire to control. They generally show a loose-eye and have a great amount of force while working well off the stock. They make much use of their ability to intimidate.

The Rottweiler often carries the head on an even plane with the back or carries the head up but with the neck and shoulders lowered. Some females lower the entire front end slightly when using eye. Males also do this when working far off the stock in an open field. This is rarely seen in males when working in confined spaces such as stock yards.

The Rottweiler has a reasonably good natural balance, force-barks when necessary, and when working cattle uses a very intimidating charge. There is a natural change in forcefulness when herding sheep. When working cattle it may use its body and shoulders and for this reason should be used on horned stock with caution.

The Rottweiler, when working cattle, searches out the dominant animal and challenges it. Upon proving its control over that animal it settles back and tend to its work.

Some growers have found that Rottweilers are especially suited to move stubborn stock that simply ignore Border Collies, Kelpies, and others. Rottweilesr use their bodies to physically force the stubborn animal to do its bidding if necessary.

When working with sheep the Rottweiler shows a gathering/fetching style and reams directions easily. It drives sheep with ease.

In some cases Rottweilers have begun herding cattle without any experience at all.

If worked on the same stock for any length of time the Rottweiler tends to develop a bond with the stock and will become quite affectionate with them as long as they do as it says.

Health

Rottweilers are a relatively healthy, disease-free breed. As with most large breeds, hip dysplasia can be a problem. For this reason the various Rottweiler breed clubs have had x-ray testing regimes in place for many years. A reputable breeder will have the hips and elbows of all breeding stock x-rayed and read by a recognised specialist, and will have paperwork to prove it.

They will also have certificates that their breeding animals do not have entropion or ectropion and that they have full and complete dentition with a scissor bite.

As with any breed, hereditary conditions occur in some lines. Because of recent overbreeding, cancer has become one of the leading causes of early death in Rottweilers.

If overfed or under exercised, Rottweilers are prone to obesity. Some of the consequences of obesity can be very serious, including arthritis, breathing difficulties, diabetes, heart failure, reproductive problems, skin disease, reduced resistance to disease and overheating caused by the thick jacket of fat under the skin.

Gallery

References

- American Kennel Club Herding Regulations. The full document is available at AKC.org [1]
- Australian National Kennel Council, Extended Breed Standard of the Rottweiler. Available online at ANKC.org.au [2]
- Blackmore, Joan. A Dog Owners Guide to the Rottweiler
- Brace, Andrew H. (Ed), The Ultimate Rottweiler, Ringpress Books, Surrey, 2003. ISBN 1-86054-263-8
- Coren,Stanley. The Intelligence of Dogs, University of British Columbia, Vancouver. (1994).
- Chardets: Know your Rottweiler
- Fédération Cynologique Internationale-Standard N° 147/ 19. 06. 2000 / GB The Rottweiler. Translated by - Mrs C. Seidler Country of Origin – Germany.
- Kaneene JB, Mostosky UV, Miller R. Update of a retrospective cohort study of changes in hip joint phenotype of dogs evaluated by the OFA in the United States, 1989-2003. Vet Surg 2009;38:398-405, Interscience.wiley.com [3], abstract
- National Dog - The Ringleader Way, Volume 12 Number 1 & 2, Jan/Feb 2009 Breed Feature "Bernese Mountain Dogs, Leonbergers & Rottweilers".
- Pettengell, Jim. The Rottweiler
- Pienkoss, Adolf. The Rottweiler, 3rd revised and updated edition, Internationale Foederation der Rottweilerfreunde (IFR) Wilhelmitenstr. 15a, 46354 Borken, Germany, 2008

- Price, Les. Rottweilers: an owner's companion. Macmillan Publishing Company, New York 1991. ISBN 0-87605-297-9
- Schanzle, Manfred, Studies In The Breed History Of The Rottweiler. German edition Published by Allgemeiner Deutscher Rottweiller - Klub (ADRK) E.V. 1967 English edition published jointly by Colonial Rottweiler Club & Medallion Rottweiler Club - Sept 1969. 1981 Printing (updated) - Published by Powderhorn Press 3320 Wonderview Plaza, Hollywood, CA90068.
- Yrjola, J.A.U. & Tikka, Elvi. Our Friend the Rottweiler.

St. Bernard (dog)

The **St. Bernard Dog** is a very large breed of dog, a working dog from the Swiss Alps, originally bred for rescue. The breed has become famous through tales of alpine rescues, as well as for its large size.

Appearance

The St. Bernard is a very large dog with a large head. The longest recorded dog was 42 inches (107 cm) tall, 35 inches (89 cm) at the shoulders, and 102 inches (2.59 m) long and weighed 220 lb (100 kg), The average weight of the breed is between 140 and 264 lb (64–120 kg) or more and the approximate height at the withers is 27½ inches to 35½ inches (70 to 90 cm). The coat can be either smooth or rough, with the smooth coat close and flat. The rough coat is dense but flat, and more profuse around the neck and legs. The coat is typically a red colour with white, or sometimes a mahogany brindle with white. Black shading is usually found on the face and ears. The tail is long and heavy, hanging low with the end turned up slightly. The dark eyes should have naturally tight lids, with "haws only slightly visible".

History

The ancestors of the St. Bernard share a history with the Sennenhunds, also called Swiss Mountain Dogs or Swiss Cattle Dogs, the large farm dogs of the farmers and dairymen of the Swiss Alps, which were livestock guardians, herding dogs, and draft dogs as well as hunting dogs, search and rescue dogs, and watchdogs. These dogs are thought to be descendants of molosser type dogs brought into the Alps by the ancient Romans, and the St. Bernard is recognized internationally today as one of the Molossoid breeds.

The earliest written records of the St. Bernard breed are from monks at the hospice at the Great St Bernard Pass in 1707, with paintings and drawings of the dog dating even earlier.

The most famous St. Bernard to save people at the pass was Barry (sometimes spelled Berry), who reportedly saved somewhere between 40 and 100 lives. There is a monument to Barry in the Cimetière des Chiens, and his body was preserved in the Natural History Museum in Berne.

The classic Saint Bernard looked very different from the St. Bernard of today, because avalanches killed off many of the dogs used for breeding between 1816 and 1818. Severe weather during this period led to an increased number of avalanches that killed many St. Bernards while performing rescue work. In an attempt to preserve the breed, the remaining St. Bernards were crossed with Newfoundlands brought from the Colony of Newfoundland in the 1850s, and so lost much of their use as rescue dogs in the snowy climate of the alps because the long fur they inherited would freeze and weigh them down.

The Swiss St. Bernard Club was founded in Basel on March 15, 1884. The St. Bernard was the very first breed entered into the Swiss Stud Book in 1884, and the breed standard was finally approved in 1888. Since then, the breed has been a Swiss national dog.

Naming

The name "St. Bernard" originates from traveler's hospice on the often treacherous St. Bernard Pass in the Western Alps between Switzerland and Italy, where the name was passed to the local dogs. The pass, the lodge, and the dogs are named for Bernard of Menthon, the 11th century monk who established the station.

"St. Bernard" wasn't in widespread use until the middle of the 19th century. The dogs were called "Saint Dogs", "Noble Steeds", "Alpenmastiff", or "Barry Dogs" before that time. They were also used for rescuing people from the Alps.

Related breeds

The breed is strikingly similar to the English Mastiff and Newfoundland. This can be attributed to a common shared ancestry with the Alpine Mastiff and the Tibetan Mastiff. It is suspected that these breeds were used to redevelop each other to combat the threat of their extinction after World War II.

The four Sennenhund breeds, the Grosser Schweizer Sennenhund (Greater Swiss Mountain Dog), the Berner Sennenhund, (Bernese Mountain Dog), the Appenzeller Sennenhund, (Appenzeller), and the Entlebucher Sennenhund (Entlebucher Mountain Dog) are similar in appearance and share the same location and history, but are tricolour rather than red and white.

Kennel Club recognition

The St. Bernard is recognised internationally by the Fédération Cynologique Internationale as a Molosser in Group 2, Section 2. The breed is recognised by The Kennel Club (UK), the Canadian Kennel Club, and the American Kennel Club in the Working Dog breed group. The United Kennel Club (US) places the breed in the Guardian Dog Group. The New Zealand Kennel Club and the Australian National Kennel Council place the breed in the Utility Group

Activities

St. Bernard dogs are no longer used for alpine rescues, but do participate in a variety of dog sports including carting and weight pulling. A St. Bernard holds the world record in strength: in 2008, a St. Bernard was recorded to pull over 2 tons.

Health

The very fast growth rate and the weight of a St. Bernard can lead to very serious deterioration of the bones if the dog does not get proper food and exercise. Many dogs are genetically affected by hip dysplasia or elbow dysplasia. Osteosarcoma (bone cancer) has been shown to be hereditary in the breed.

St. Bernards are susceptible to eye disorders called entropion and ectropion, in which the eyelid turns in or out. The breed standard indicates that this is a major fault.

The breed is also susceptible to epilepsy and seizures, a heart disease called dilated cardiomyopathy, and eczema.

Due to the likelihood of health problems in later years, the average lifespan for a St. Bernard is around 8 years. St. Bernards may live beyond 10 years but those dogs are rare.

Temperament

St. Bernards, like all very large dogs, must be well socialized with people and other dogs in order to prevent fearfulness and any possible aggression or territoriality. The biggest threat to small children is being knocked over by this breed's larger size. Overall they are a loyal and affectionate breed, and if socialized are very friendly and are occasionally avoided because of their slobber.

Due to its large adult size, it is essential that proper training and socialization begin while the St. Bernard is still a puppy, so as to avoid the difficulties that normally accompany training large animals. An unruly St. Bernard may present problems for even a strong adult, so control needs to be asserted from the beginning of the dog's training. While generally not as aggressive as dogs bred for protection, a St. Bernard may bark at strangers, and their size makes them good deterrents against possible intruders.

Notability

Record size

St. Bernards were exported to England in the mid 1800s, where they were bred with mastiffs to create an even larger dog. Plinlimmon, a famous St. Bernard of the time, was measured at 95 kg (210 lbs) and 87.5 cm (34 1/2ins), and was sold to an American for $7000. Commercial pressure encouraged carelessly breeding ever larger dogs until "the dogs became so gross that they had difficulties in getting from one end of a show ring to another".

The world's heaviest and largest dog in known history is claimed to be a Saint Bernard named Benedictine, which measured 9 ft in length and weighed 162 kg (357 lbs). This claim, although unsubstantiated by any records organization, would surpass Zorba, the largest English mastiff on record, in both length and weight. Zorba measured 8 feet, 3 inches long and weighed 343 lb.

In media

St. Bernards are often portrayed, especially in old live action comedies such as *Swiss Miss*, the TV series *Topper*, and classic cartoons wearing small barrels of brandy around their necks. A frequent joke in old MGM and Warner Brothers shorts is to depict the dogs as compulsive alcoholics who engage in frequent nips from their own casks. This was supposedly used to warm the victims that the dogs found. The monks of the St. Bernard Hospice deny that any St. Bernard has ever carried casks or small barrels around their necks; they believe that the origin of the image is an early painting. The monks did keep casks around for photographs by tourists.

A *Punch* magazine cartoon from 1949 depicts a man with a St. Bernard and several puppies, all of which are wearing neck casks. The man explains, "Of course, I only breed them for the brandy."

The 1981 Stephen King novel *Cujo* portrays a rabid and crazed St. Bernard that terrorizes the residents of the fictional town of Castle Rock, Maine.

The 1992 comedy film *Beethoven* featured a large, friendly but troublesome St. Bernard and, in later sequels, his mate and their brood of unruly pups. According to the producers of the sequel Beethoven's 2nd, the St. Bernards used in the film grew so fast during filming that over 100 St. Bernard puppies were cast to potray the sequel's four puppies (Tchaikovsky, Chubby, Dolly, and Mo).

Famous St. Bernards

- Schotzie & Schotzie "02", beloved pets and mascots of Cincinnati Reds' owner Marge Schott
- Barry, famous Alpine rescue dog
- Bolivar, Donald Duck's pet
- Cujo, a fictional portrayal of a rabid St. Bernard by Stephen King
- Nanna, from various *Peter Pan* movies (but originally a Newfoundland in the text)
- Buck, from Jack London's *The Call of the Wild*, is half St. Bernard
- Gumbo, team mascot for the New Orleans Saints
- Neil, the martini-slurping St. Bernard of George and Marion Kerby in *Topper*
- Beethoven, the 1992 movie *Beethoven*, and multiple sequels
- Bamse, a Norwegian dog honoured for exploits during World War II memorial statue in Montrose, Scotland where he died in 1944
- Båtsman, a St. Bernard in Astrid Lindgren's story *Vi på Saltkråkan*
- Schnorbitz, on-stage partner of British comedian Bernie Winters during his later career

- Gumbo, Bradley Brannings pet dog on *EastEnders*
- Wallace (currently Wallace VI), mascot of The Canadian Scottish Regiment (Princess Mary's)
- Bernie, mascot of the Colorado Avalanche

Legends

The famous Barry found a small boy in the snow and persuaded the boy to climb on his back, and then carried the boy to safety.

A St Bernard is often credited with being the dog that helped save Manchester United, currently one of the world's largest football clubs, from financial ruin. The legend goes that in 1902 when the club owed sizable debts, the then captain Harry Stafford was showing off his prized St Bernard at a fund-raiser for the club when he was approached by a wealthy brewery owner, J.H.Davis, who enquired to buy the dog. Harry Stafford refused the offer but managed to convince him to buy the club thus saving Manchester United from going bankrupt.

See also

- Great St Bernard Pass
- Great St Bernard Hospice
- Dog sports

Samoyed (dog)

The **Samoyed** dog (pronounced or ;) takes its name from the Samoyedic peoples of Siberia. An alternate name for the breed, especially in Europe, is **Bjelkier**. These nomadic reindeer herders bred the fluffy, white dogs to help with the herding, to pull sleds when they moved.

Appearance

The average lifespan for a Samoyed is 12 to 16 years. Being a working breed, they have high stamina.

They share a common resemblance with an American Eskimo dog.

Size

Males typically weigh between 20-32.5 kg (55-71 lbs) and stand at a height of 54–60 cm (21–24 in) , while females typically weigh 17–25 kg(40-55 lbs) and stand at a height of 50–56 cm (19–22 in) .

Eyes

Samoyed eyes are usually black or brown and are almond in shape. Blue or other color eyes can occur but are not allowed in the show ring.

Ears

Samoyed ears are thick and covered with fur, triangular in shape, and erect. They are almost always white but can occasionally have a light brown tint, usually around the tips of ears.

Tail

The Samoyed tail is one of the breed's more distinguishing features. Like the Alaskan Malamute, their tail is carried curled over their backs; however, unlike the Malamute, the Samoyed tail is held actually touching the back. It should not be a tight curl or held "flag" like, it should be carried lying over the back and to one side. In cold weather, Samoyeds may sleep with their tails over their noses to provide additional warmth. Almost all Samoyeds will allow their tails to fall when they are relaxed and at ease, as when being stroked or while eating, but will return their tails to a curl when more alert.

NZKC Standard: Tail: Long and profuse, carried over the back when alert; sometimes dropped when at rest.

UK Kennel Club Standard : Tail : Long and Profusely coated, carried over the back and to side when alert, sometimes dropped when at rest.

Coat

Samoyeds have a dense, double layer coat. The topcoat contains long, coarse, and straight guard hairs, which appear white but have a hint of silver coloring. This top layer keeps the undercoat relatively clean and free of debris. The under layer, or undercoat, consists of a dense, soft, and short fur that keeps the dog warm. The undercoat is typically shed heavily once or twice a year, and this seasonal process is sometimes referred to as "blowing coat". This does not mean the Samoyed will only shed during that time however; fine hairs (versus the dense clumps shed during seasonal shedding) will be shed all year round, and have a tendency to stick to cloth and float in the air. The standard Samoyed may come in a mixture of biscuit and white coloring, although pure white and all biscuit dogs aren't uncommon. Males typically have larger ruffs than females.

Temperament

Samoyeds' friendly disposition makes them poor guard dogs; an aggressive Samoyed is rare. With their tendency to bark, however, they can be diligent watch dogs, barking whenever something approaches their territory. Samoyeds are excellent companions, especially for small children or even other dogs, and they remain playful into old age. When Samoyeds become bored they may begin to dig. With their sled dog heritage, a Samoyed is not averse to pulling things, and an untrained Samoyed has no problem pulling its owner on a leash rather than walking alongside. Samoyeds were also used to herd reindeer. They will instinctively act as herd dogs, and when playing with children, especially, will often attempt to turn and move them in a different direction. The breed is characterized by an alert and happy expression which has earned the nicknames "Sammy smile" and "smiley dog."

Health

Samoyed Hereditary Glomerulopathy

Samoyeds can be affected by a genetic disease known as "Samoyed Hereditary Glomerulopathy", a renal disease. The disease is known to be caused by an X-linked dominant faulty allele and therefore the disease is more severe in male Samoyeds. Carrier females do develop mild symptoms after 2–3 months of age, but do not go on to develop renal failure. The disease is caused by a defect in the structure of the type-IV collagen fibrils of the glomerular basement membrane. As a consequence, the collagen fibrils of the glomerular basement membrane are unable to form cross-links, so the structural integrity is weakened and the membrane is more susceptible to "wear-and-tear" damage. As the structure of the basement membrane begins to degenerate, plasma proteins are lost in the urine and symptoms begin to appear. Affected males appear healthy for the first 3 months of life, but then symptoms start to appear and worsen as the disease progresses: the dog becomes lethargic and muscle wastage occurs, as a result of proteinuria. From 3 months of age onwards, a reduced glomerular filtration rate is detected, indicative of progressive renal failure. Death from renal failure usually occurs by 15 months of age.

As yet there is no genetic screening test available for Samoyed Hereditary Glomerulopathy. If a carrier female is mated with a healthy stud dog, the female offspring have a 50% chance of being carriers for the disease, and any male offspring have a 50% chance of being affected by the disease.

Other health concerns

Hip dysplasia is also a concern for Samoyeds as are eye problems such as cataracts and glaucoma and other retinal problems. Like other purebred dogs, Samoyeds are prone to diabetes and other diseases if their owners are not careful. Life expectancy is about 12–15 years.

History

The Samoyed was used for sledding, herding, guarding and keeping their owners warm.

Fridtjof Nansen believed that the use of sled dogs was the only effective way to explore the north and used Samoyeds on his polar expeditions. His plan to feed the weaker dogs to the stronger ones as they died during the expedition ultimately consumed nearly all of his dogs.

Roald Amundsen used a team of sled dogs led by a Samoyed named Etah on the first expedition to reach the South Pole.

Recent DNA analysis of the breed has led to the Samoyed being included amongst the fourteen most ancient dog breeds [1], along with Siberian Huskies, Alaskan Malamutes, the Chow Chow, and 10 others of a diverse geographic background. The first Samoyed was brought to United States by fur traders in 1906. The Samoyeds have been bred and trained for at least 3,000 years. Like the former two other dog breeds, the Samoyed also has a wolf-like appearance, and has also sometimes crossbred to wolves to produce a wolf-dog hybrid.

Miscellaneous

- Shed Samoyed fur is sometimes used as an alternative to wool in knitting, with hypoallergenic properties and a texture similar to angora. The fur is sometimes also used for the creation of flys for fly fishing. Samoyed fur sweaters have been reported to handle temperatures well below freezing.
- Samoyeds are rarely used for *highly* competitive dogsled racing because of the emergence of breeds bred specifically for the sport such as the Alaskan Husky, however they are still fully capable of racing competitively or pulling sleds recreationally if desired.
- Samoyeds are very rarely used for everyday herding work on farms, as breeds with higher herding drives such as Border Collies or Australian Shepherds are more practical to use for this job. Many Samoyeds however, do retain the herding instinct and occasionally have been used to herd sheep, goats, and ducks competitively and recreationally.

Famous Samoyeds

- Kaifas and Suggen, the lead dogs for Fridtjof Nansen's North Pole expedition.
- Etah, the lead dog for Roald Amundsen's expedition to the South Pole, the first to reach the pole.
- Soichiro is the name of a Samoyed that belonged to one of the main characters in the popular Japanese anime, *Maison Ikkoku*. He was featured prominently throughout most of the series, and became a major character in his own right, often serving as comic relief.
- Samoyeds serve as the sled dogs of Stone Fox in the book of the same name.
- Xiah Junsu, member of South Korean boy band TVXQ, owns a Samoyed named Shaki.
- Mush was the name of the Samoyed dog owned by Karen Carpenter of the popular music group The Carpenters.

External links

- Samoyed Club of America website [2]
- The Samoyed Club Inc. New Zealand [3]
- Organization for the Working Samoyed [4]
- Homepages of the Samoyed dog, with links to all major national organizations. [5]
- Samoyed Club of South Australia Inc [6]
- Keftiu Samoyeds [7]

Siberian Husky

The **Siberian Husky** (, *Sibirskiy haski,* "Siberian Dog") is a medium-size, dense-coat working dog breed that originated in eastern Siberia. The breed belongs to the Spitz genetic family. It is recognizable by its thickly furred double coat, sickle tail, erect triangular ears, and distinctive markings

Huskies are an active, energetic, and resilient breed whose ancestors came from the extremely cold and harsh environment of the Siberian Arctic. Siberian Huskies were bred by the Chukchi of Northeastern Asia to pull heavy loads long distances through difficult conditions. The dogs were imported into Alaska during the Nome Gold Rush and later spread into the United States and Canada. They were initially sent to Alaska and Canada as sled dogs but rapidly acquired the status of family pets and show dogs.

History

The Siberian Husky, Samoyed, and Alaskan Malamute are all breeds directly descended from the original "sled dog." Recent DNA analysis confirms that this is one of the oldest breeds of dog.

The name "Husky" does not mean that these dogs are burly, thick, fat, or overweight. "Husky" originated as a mutation of the term "Eskie," a derogatory name used by the Europeans to describe the Inuit people whom they met when they first made expeditions into the Arctic.

Breeds descending from the Eskimo dog were once found throughout the Northern Hemisphere from Siberia to Canada, Alaska, Greenland, Labrador, and Baffin Island.

With the help of Siberian Huskies, entire tribes of peoples were able not only to survive, but to push forth into *terra incognita.* Admiral Robert Peary of the United States Navy was aided by this breed during his expeditions in search of the North Pole.

Dogs from the Anadyr River and surrounding regions were imported into Alaska from 1908 (and for the next two decades) during the gold rush for use as sled dogs, especially in the "All-Alaska Sweepstakes," a 408-mile (657 km) distance dog sled race from Nome to Candle and back. Smaller, faster and more enduring than the 100- to 120-pound (45 to 54 kg) freighting dogs then in general use, they immediately dominated the Nome Sweepstakes. Leonhard Seppala, the foremost breeder of Siberian Huskies of the time, participated in competitions from 1909 to the mid 1920s.

On February 3, 1925 Gunnar Kaasen was first in the 1925 serum run to Nome to deliver diphtheria serum from Nenana over 600 miles to Nome. This was a group effort by several sled dog teams and mushers. The Iditarod Trail Sled Dog Race commemorates this famous delivery. The event is also loosely depicted in the 1995 animated film *Balto*, as the name of Gunnar Kaasen's lead dog in his sled team was named Balto, although unlike the real dog, Balto the character was portrayed as half wolf in the film. In honor of this lead dog a bronze statue was erected at Central Park in New York City. The plaque upon it is inscribed,

Dedicated to the indomitable spirit of the sled dogs that relayed antitoxin six hundred miles over rough ice, across treacherous waters, through Arctic blizzards from Nenana to the relief of stricken Nome in the winter of 1925. Endurance · Fidelity · Intelligence

In 1930 the last Siberians were exported as the Soviet government closed the borders of Siberia to external trade. The same year saw recognition of the Siberian Husky by the American Kennel Club. Nine years later the breed was first registered in Canada. Today's Siberian Huskies registered in North America are largely the descendants of the 1930 Siberia imports and of Leonhard Seppala's dogs. Seppala owned a kennel in Nenana before moving to New England. Arthur Walden, owner of Chinook Kennels of Wonalancet, New Hampshire, was by far the most prominent breeder of Siberian Huskies. The foundation of his kennel stock came directly from Alaska, and Seppala's kennel.

As the breed was beginning to come to prominence, in 1933 Navy Rear Admiral Richard E. Byrd brought about 50 Siberian Huskies with him on an expedition in which Byrd hoped to journey around the 16,000-mile coast of Antarctica. Many of the dogs were trained at Chinook Kennels in New Hampshire. Called Operation Highjump, the historic trek proved the worth of the Siberian Husky due to its compact size and greater speeds. Siberian Huskies also served in the United States Army's Arctic Search and Rescue Unit of the Air Transport Command during World War II.

Appearance

Siberian Huskies share many outward similarities with the Alaskan Malamute as well as many other Spitz breeds such as the Samoyed, which has a comparable history to the Huskies. They come in a variety of colors and patterns, usually with white paws and legs, facial markings, and tail tip. The most common colors are black and white, copper-red and white, gray and white, and pure white, though many individuals have blondish or piebald spotting. Striking masks, spectacles, and other facial markings occur in wide variety. They tend to have a wolf-like appearance.

Eyes

The American Kennel Club describes the Husky's eyes as "an almond shape, moderately spaced and set slightly obliquely." The eyes of a Siberian Husky are ice-blue, dark blue, amber, or brown. In some individual dogs, one eye may be brown and the other blue (complete heterochromia), or one or both eyes may be "parti-colored," that is, half brown and half blue (partial heterochromia). All of these eye color combinations are considered acceptable by the American Kennel Club.

Coat

The Siberian Husky's coat is thicker than that of most breeds of dogs, comprising two layers: a dense undercoat and a longer topcoat of short, straight guard hairs. It protects the dogs effectively against harsh Arctic winters, but the coat also reflects heat in the summer. It is able to withstand temperatures as low as −50 °C to −60 °C. The undercoat is often absent during shedding.Their thick coats require weekly grooming. Long guard hair is not desirable and is considered a fault.

Nose

Show-quality dogs are preferred to have neither pointed nor square noses. The nose is black in gray dogs, tan in black dogs, liver in copper-colored dogs, and may be flesh-colored in white dogs. In some instances, Siberian Huskies can exhibit what is called "snow nose" or "winter nose." This condition is called hypopigmentation in animals. "Snow nose" is acceptable in the show ring.

Size

The breed standard indicates that the males of the breed are ideally between tall at the withers and weighing between . Females are smaller, growing to between tall at the withers and weighing between .

Behavior

The Siberian Husky has been described as a behavioral representative of the domestic dog's forebearer, the wolf, exhibiting a wide range of its ancestors' behavior. They are known to howl rather than bark. Hyperactivity, displaying as an overactive hunting drive, a characteristic of kenneled dogs, is often noticeable in dogs released from their captive environment for exercise — a behavior welcome in hunting dogs but not in the family pet. The frequency of kenneled Siberian Huskies, especially for racing purposes, is rather high, as attributed through the history of the breed in North America. They are affectionate with people, but independent. A fifteen-minute daily obedience training class will serve well for Siberian Huskies. Siberians need consistent training and do well with a positive reinforcement training program. They rank 45th in Stanley Coren's *The Intelligence of Dogs,* being of average working/obedience intelligence. They tend to run because they were at first bred to be sled dogs. Owners are advised to exercise caution when letting their Siberian Husky off the leash as the dog is likely to be miles away before looking around and realizing their owner is nowhere in sight. They also get bored easily, so playing with toys or throwing the ball at least once a day is essential. Failure to give them the attention or proper exercise they need can result in unwanted behavior, such as excessive howling, marking, chewing on furniture, or crying. This dog is sometimes called "the clown of the dogs" after its love to play like a puppy all through its life.

Intelligence

Siberian Huskies are highly intelligent, which allows them to excel in obedience trials, though many clubs would like to keep the Husky's instinct by doing sled-racing. However, because of their intelligence, they can easily become bored and may stop listening to commands. Many dog trainers usually attempt to avoid this behavior by keeping them busy with new activities. Also due in part to their intelligence, Huskies tend to be very observant on the actions of people around them and have been known to mimic common household activities such as turning on lights with their paws and opening doors with their canines. Some undesirable behaviors they can exhibit include opening refrigerators (and eating the food inside), climbing fences or digging tunnels in the backyard to escape. These behaviors can be prevented if the dog is given enough activity to occupy it.

Health

Siberian Huskies, with proper care, have a typical lifespan ranging from twelve to fifteen years. Health issues in the breed are mainly genetic such as seizures and defects of the eye (juvenile cataracts, corneal dystrophy, and progressive retinal atrophy). Hip dysplasia is not often found in this breed; however, as with many medium or larger-sized canines, it can occur. The Orthopedic Foundation for Animals currently has the Siberian Husky ranked 148th out of a possible 153 breeds at risk for hip dysplasia, with only two percent of tested Siberian Huskies showing dysplasia.

Siberian Huskies used for sled racing may also be prone to other ailments, such as gastric disease, bronchitis or bronchopulmonary ailments ("ski asthma"), and gastric erosions or ulcerations.

Working Siberians

Siberian Huskies are still used as sled dogs in sled dog racing. Siberians are still popular in races restricted to purebreds and are faster than other pure sled dog breeds such as the Samoyed and the slower but much stronger Alaskan Malamute. Today the breed tends to divide along lines of "racing" Siberians and "show" Siberians. Racing Siberians tend to have more leg to enable them more reach when running. Show Siberians tend to be a bit smaller.

Apart from sled racing, they are very popular for recreational mushing and are also used for skijoring (one to three dogs pulling a skier) and European ski-hi. A few owners use them for dog-packing and hiking.

In the United Kingdom and Australia, due to the lack of snow, Siberian Huskies are raced on forest tracks using specially designed scooters with two wheels for one or two dogs, or three-wheeled rigs for three or more dogs. This sledding can be a good hobby and sport for a pet Husky. There are many clubs across the world for sledding.

Famous Siberians

Siberians gained in popularity with the story of the 1925 serum run to Nome, which made dogs Balto and Togo famous.

Several purebred Siberian Huskies portrayed Diefenbaker, the "half-wolf" companion to RCMP Constable Benton Fraser in the CBS/Alliance Atlantis TV series Due South.

See also

- Alaskan Husky
- Alaskan Malamute
- Canadian Eskimo Dog
- Laika (dog breed)

External links

- It's a Husky Thing- Online Forum for Husky Owners [1]

Standard Schnauzer

The **Standard Schnauzer** is the original breed of the three breeds of Schnauzer, and despite its wiry coat and general appearance, is not related to the British terriers. Rather, its origins are in old herding and guard breeds of Europe. Generally classified as a working or utility dog, this versatile breed is a robust, squarely built, medium-sized dog with aristocratic bearing. It was a popular subject of painters Sir Joshua Reynolds, Albrecht Dürer and Rembrandt.

Standard Schnauzers are either pepper-and-salt or black in color, and are known for exhibiting many of the "ideal" traits of any breed. These include high intelligence, agility, alertness, reliability, strength, endurance, and affection. Standard Schnauzers are one of the oldest breeds with over 500 years of history. This breed of dog has been very popular in Europe, specifically Germany where it originated. The breed was first exhibited at a show in Hanover in 1879. They are majestic and regal in the show ring, and have taken top honors in many shows including the prestigious "Best in Show at Westminster Kennel Club" in 1997.

History

Schnauzers are originally a German breed, descended during the Middle Ages from herding, ratting and guardian breeds. They may be most closely related to German Pinschers, and the spitz-type breeds. Dogs very similar to today's schnauzers existed in the Middle Ages. They were portrayed in paintings, statues and tapestries, including by artists Rembrandt, Dürer and Reynolds. Initially a dog of the peasant farmer, in the 19th century this breed captured the interest of the German dog fancier and they began to be bred to a standard.

The Schnauzer breed takes its name from one of its kind, a show dog winner by that name, "Schnauzer", at the 1879 Hanover Show in Germany. The word *Schnauzer* (from the German word for 'snout') appeared for the first time in 1842 when used as a synonym for the Wire-haired *Pinscher* (the name under which the breed first competed at dog shows). The Standard Schnauzer is the original Schnauzer from which the Miniature and Giant breeds were developed in the late 19th century. They have been shown from the 1870s onwards and first appeared in the United States about 1900.

The Standard Schnauzer has been used throughout modern history in various roles. The Red Cross used the dogs for guard duty during World War I. Both German and American police departments put the dogs to work as well. Several Standards have been used in the USA for drug and bomb detection, and also as search-and-rescue dogs.

The modern Standard Schnauzer excels at obedience, agility, tracking, herding, therapy work and, in Germany, schutzhund. Despite being a very popular pet in Europe, the Standard Schnauzer has never gained wide popularity in North America. For the past 20 years, the American Kennel Club has registered only ~540 Standard Schnauzer puppies a year. Compare that to the Labrador retriever at nearly ~100,000 puppies a year and it is clear the Standard Schnauzer has a very small - but loyal - fan club.

Appearance

Distinguished by their long beards and eyebrows, Standard Schnauzers are always pepper and salt or less commonly black in color, with a stiff and wiry fur coat on the body similar to that of other wirehaired breeds such as many breeds of terrier. Their hair will perpetually grow in length without properly shedding, but contrary to popular belief Standard Schnauzers are not hypo-allergenic and they all shed to some degree. The more wiry - and correct and weather-resistant - the coat, the more that the coat will shed, though the hair dropped from a single dog is said to be nearly unnoticeable.

Twice a year, when most other breeds of dog are shedding their coat, a Schnauzer's coat will become dull and relatively easy to pull out and is said to have 'blown'. At this point the coat can be stripped or pulled out by hand and a new wire coat will re-grow in its place. Stripping is not painful for the dog and can be performed at any stage of hair growth although it is easier to do when the coat is 'blown'.

Alternatively, the coat can be regularly clipped with shears. Clipping as opposed to stripping results in a loss of the wiry texture and some of the fullness of the coat. Dogs with clipped fur no longer 'blow' their coat but the coat loses its wiry texture and becomes soft. The fur of clipped dogs tends to be more prone to tangling and knots, particularly when long, and is duller in color than that of stripped coats. In the case of the salt and pepper Schnauzers, the characteristic banded color of the hair is completely lost when maintained through clipping; each shaft of hair becomes entirely gray rather than being banded with multiple shades of gray, white, and black.

Clipping is most common in the US as it can be difficult to locate a professional willing to hand strip as the process is quite labor intensive. In Europe it is very uncommon to see a wire-coated dog which is clipped. It may not be possible to hand strip a poor quality coat, i.e. one that is soft in texture, but soft coats, while relatively common in pet quality Miniature Schnauzers, is not a widespread problem in Standards.

Regardless of whether the body of the coat is stripped or clipped the 'furnishings' or longer hair on the legs and face must be scissored or clipped regularly and require daily brushing to remain free of potentially painful mats. Whether a Schnauzer is stripped or clipped, his coat requires a great deal of grooming. In most cases this means an owner must either take care to learn the required grooming - for which the dog's breeder should be a great resource - or the owner must take their dog in for regular, often expensive, trips to a grooming salon.

Inside the US and Canada, ears and tail and dewclaws are typically docked as a puppy. Veterinarians or experienced breeders will cut tails and dewclaws between 3 and 7 days of age. Tails are traditionally docked to around three vertebrate. Ear cropping is usually performed at about 10 weeks of age in a veterinary clinic. Many breeders inside North America have begun to crop only those puppies retained for show purposes, or those puppies whose owners request it. There is still somewhat of a bias against natural ears in the North American show ring. However, there is a growing sentiment among breeders and judges that both ear types are equally show-worthy, and many North American show breeders enjoy both cropped and natural eared dogs in their kennels. However, unlike in Europe, the majority of North American breeders believe that the choice of whether to cut ears and/or tails should continue to remain with the breeders and owners. Outside of North America, most Standard Schnauzers retain both their natural ears and tail as docking is now prohibited by law in many countries.

Temperament

The smallest of the working breeds, the Standard schnauzer makes loyal family dog with guardian instincts. Most will protect their home from uninvited visitors with a deep and robust bark. Originally a German farmdog, they adapt well to any climatic condition, including cold winters. In general, they typically are good with children and were once known in Germany as "kinderwachters". If properly trained and socialized early to different ages, races, and temperaments of people, they can be very patient and tolerant in any situation. Like other working dogs, Standard Schnauzers require a fairly strong-willed owner that can be consistent and firm with training and commands.

Standard Schnauzers also widely known to be intelligent and easy to train. They have been called "the dog with a human brain", and in Stanley Coren's book The Intelligence of Dogs, they are rated 18th out of 80 breeds on the ability to learn new commands and to obey known commands. Standard Schnauzers are extremely versatile, excelling at dog sports such as agility, obedience, tracking, Disc dog, Flyball and herding. Members of the breed have been used in the last 30 years in the United States as for bomb detection, search and rescue, and skin and lung cancer-detection.

Like most working dogs, Standard Schnauzers will be rambunctious until about the age of two; and lots of exercise will keep them busy. Owners must be prepared to mentally and physically stimulate their Schnauzer every day, even into their old age. Like other high-intelligence breeds, a bored Schnauzer is a destructive Schnauzer.

According to the Standard Schnauzer Club of America, "The Standard Schnauzer is considered a high-energy dog. They need ample exercise not only for physical well-being, but also for emotional well-being. The minimum amount an adult dog should get is the equivalent of a one long walk a day. This walk should be brisk enough to keep the dog at a steady trotting pace in order to keep the dog in prime physical condition. The Standard Schnauzer puppy is constantly exploring, learning and testing his limits. As adults, they are always ready for a walk in the woods, a ride in the car, a training session or any other activity that allows them to be with their owner. This is a breed that knows how to be on the alert, even when relaxing by the feet of their owner.

Health

Overall, the Standard Schnauzer is a very healthy breed. The 2008 health survey done by the Standard Schnauzer Club of America revealed that roughly only 1% of dogs surveyed had serious health issues. The final, full report can be found here [1] but a general summery is as follows:

- Data was collected for 10-15% of eligible dogs;
- Median life span was 12.9 years
- Only a few serious diseases were noted;
- Potentially serious conditions affect less than 1% of dogs
- Apparent progress has been made in reducing the incidence of hip dysplasia

The two major hereditary within the breed are: hip dysplasia and hereditary eye disease. Both problems can be tested for and identified in breeding stock before they pass the trait onto the next generation, so the Standard Schnauzer Club of America [2] recommends that every kennel test their breeding stock for hip and eye problems before breeding and to breed only healthy animals.

However, it is entirely up to breeders whether they choose to health test their animals and whether they choose use animals for breeding despite knowing they have tested positive for carrying a genetic disease. The SSCA [2] also encourages all potential buyers to ask their breeder for up to date OFA and

CERF certifications of the parent dogs before buying a puppy.

The Orthopedic Foundation for Animals found at www.offa.org [3] keeps a record of purebred animals that have passed an x-ray screening for hip dysplasia. Dogs must be a minimum of two years old to be OFA tested. The OFA results reported in the 2008 SSCA [2] Health Survey [1] are as follows:

OFA Hip Rating	Number of Dogs	Percent of Tested Dogs
Excellent	50	9.7%
Good	387	73.4%
Fair	70	13.2%
Poor	9	1.7%

The cost of OFA testing is relatively high (about 150-200 USD per dog per year) and born directly by breeders. OFA testing is not required for AKC registration of breeding stock or their offspring so the benefits of a good OFA test scores are more indirect and long range for individual breeders while a poor results represent a direct negative impact. Responsible buyers looking to buy from responsible breeders should only choose puppies from a litter where both parents have current OFA test certificates and scores of "excellent", "good", "fair".

The Canine Eye Registration Foundation is a registry for purebred breeding stock who have been certified free of any hereditary eye disease: results for this test can also be found at the OFA website. Dogs must be examined by an approved veterinarian who checks for the presence of heritable eye diseases. Testing is less inexpensive (about 20-40 USD) than OFA examinations but, like OFA testing, must be done annually to remain valid.

Famous Schnauzers

- From the AKC: "Rembrandt painted several Schnauzers, Lucas Cranach the Elder shows one in a tapestry dated 1501, and in the 18th century one appears in a canvas of the English painter Sir Joshua Reynolds. In the marketplace of Mechlinburg, Germany, is a statue of a hunter dating from the 14th century, with a Schnauzer crouching at his feet which conforms very closely to the present-day show Standard." "
- George, the cancer-sniffing Schnauzer, has received much acclaim. "
- Tramp, the street-wise mutt from Lady and the Tramp is most likely a Schnauzer-mix
- Blu, Franklin's pet blue dog in *Monica's Gang*
- Colin, dog in the UK comedy series *Spaced*, became a regular feature in the middle of the first series.
- Shunaemon. dog from Fortune Dogs

See also

- Miniature Schnauzer
- Giant Schnauzer

References

- Fogle, Bruce, DVM (2000). *The New Encyclopedia of the Dog*. Doring Kindersley (DK). ISBN 0-7894-6130-7.
- "The Standard Schnauzer", Standard Schnauzer Club of America.
- Standard Schnauzer Club of America [1]
- Forum [11]

External links

- Breed clubs
    - Standard Schnauzer Club of America [2]
    - Standard Schnauzer of Canada [2]
    - Working Riesenschnauzer Federation [3]
    - Standard Schnauzer Club [3]
    - Potomac Valley Standard Schnauzer Club - Washington DC Metro Area [4]
- Information
    - AKC: Standard Schnauzer [5]
    - Canada Guide To Dogs: Standard Schnauzer [6]
    - Standard Schnauzer Information [7]
    - Dogster: Standard Schnauzer Info and Dynamics [8]
    - Dinsdale Standard Schnauzer Info [9]
    - Dog Breed Info Center [10]
    - Yahoo Pets: Standard Schnauzer [11]
    - [12]
- Rescue
    - Standard Schnauzer Club of America: Rescue Page [13]

Tibetan Mastiff

The **Tibetan Mastiff** (Do-khyi) is a very ancient breed and type of domestic dog (*Canis lupus familiaris*) originating with nomadic cultures of Central Asia.

Names and etymology

The Tibetan Mastiff also known as Do-khyi (variously translated as "home guard", "door guard", "dog which may be tied", "dog which may be kept"), reflects its use as a guardian of herds, flocks, tents, villages, monasteries, and palaces, much as the old English ban-dog (also meaning tied dog) was a dog tied outside the home as a guardian. However, in nomad camps and in villages, the Do-khyi is traditionally allowed to run loose at night and woe be unto the stranger who walks abroad after dark.

'Bhote Kukur' in Nepali means Tibetan Dog. In Mandarin Chinese, the name is 藏獒 (Zang'Ao), which literally means Tibetan Mastiff or Tibetan "big ferocious dog". In Mongolia it is called "bankhar", meaning "guard dog". The molosser type with which the modern Tibetan Mastiff breed is purportedly linked was known across the Ancient world by many names.

Description

Appearance

Currently, some breeders differentiate between two "types" of Tibetan Mastiff: The Do-khyi and the "Tsang-khyi". The "Tsang-khyi" (which, to a Tibetan, means only "dog from Tsang") is also referred to as the "monastery type", described as generally taller, heavier, more heavily boned, with more facial wrinkling and haw than the "Do-khyi" or "nomad type". Both "types" are often produced in the same litter.

Males can reach heights up to 31+ inches (80+cm) at the withers, although the standard for the breed is typically in the 25 to 28 inch (61 to 72 cm) range. The heaviest TM on record may be one weighing over 130 kg but dogs bred in the West are more typically between 140 lb (64 kg) to 180 lb (82 kg) - especially if they are in good condition and not overweight. Certainly, the enormous dogs being produced in some Western and some Chinese kennels would have "cost" too much to keep fed to have been useful to nomads; and their questionable structure would have made them well-nigh useless as livestock guardians.

The Tibetan Mastiff is considered a primitive breed. It typically retains the instincts which would be required for it to survive in Tibet, including canine pack behavior. In addition, it is one of the few primitive dog breeds that retains a single oestrus per year instead of two, even at much lower altitudes and in much more temperate climates than its native climate. This characteristic is also found in wild canids such as the wolf. Since their oestrus usually takes place during late fall, most Tibetan Mastiff puppies are born between December and January.

Its double coat is long, subject to climate, and found in a wide variety of colors including solid black, black & tan, various shades of gold, blue/gray, chocolate brown, the rarest of all the colors being solid white.

The coat of a TM lacks the unpleasant "big dog smell" that affects many large breeds. The coat - whatever its length or color(s) - should shed dirt and odors. Although the dogs shed somewhat throughout the year, there is generally one impressive "molt" in late winter or early spring and sometimes another, lesser molt in the late summer or early fall. (Sterilization of the dog or bitch may dramatically affect the coat as to texture, density, and shedding pattern.)

Tibetan Mastiffs are shown under one standard in the West, but separated by the Indian breed standard into two varieties - Lion Head (smaller in size, exceptionally long hair from forehead to withers, creating a ruff or mane) and Tiger Head (larger in size, shorter hair)

Temperament

The native type of dog, which still exists in Tibet, and the Westernized purebred breed can vary in temperament - but so can dogs of identical breeding, within the same litter, raised in the same household. Elizabeth Schuler states, "The few individuals that remain in Tibet are ferocious and aggressive, unpredictable in their behavior, and very difficult to train. But the dogs bred by the English are obedient and attached to their masters." However, other observers have found the dogs remaining in Tibet to be quite approachable under the right circumstances - and some Western-bred dogs to be completely unapproachable.

Some Western and Asian breeders are seeking to create a replica of the legendary dog which they identify as the "true Tibetan Mastiff" or "Tsang-khyi". Some breeders appear to select primarily for appearance (great size, profuse coat, heavy wrinkling, jowls, haw) while others also select for "soft" temperament (in the West) and fierce temperament (in Asia where the dogs' "ferocity" is much vaunted and encouraged).

As a flock guardian dog in Tibet and in the West, it is tenacious in its ability to confront predators the size of wolves and leopards. As a socialized, more domestic dog, it can thrive in a spacious, fenced yard with a canine companion, but it is generally not an appropriate dog for apartment living. The Western-bred dogs are generally more easy-going, although somewhat aloof with strangers coming to the home. Through hundreds of years of selective breeding for a protective flock and family guardian, the breed has been prized for being a nocturnal sentry, keeping would-be predators and intruders at bay, barking at sounds throughout the night. Leaving a Tibetan Mastiff outside all night with neighbors nearby is not recommended. They often sleep during the day to be more active, alert and aware at night.

Like all flock guardian breeds, they are intelligent and stubborn to a fault, so obedience training is recommended (although only mildly successful with some individuals) since this is a strong-willed, powerful breed. Socialization is also critical with this breed because of their reserved nature with strangers and guardian instincts. They are excellent family dogs - for the right family. Owners must understand canine psychology and be willing and able to assume the primary leadership position. Lack of consistent, rational discipline can result in the creation of dangerous, unpredictable dogs(although this is true of virtually every dog breed).

Newspaper reports have suggested that a pair of these Mastiffs have killed tigers while guarding sheep in the highlands of Nepal.

Health

Life Expectancy Unlike most large breeds, its life expectancy is long, some 10–14 years. The breed has fewer genetic health problems than many breeds, but cases can be found of hypothyroidism, entropion, ectropion, skin problems including allergies, autoimmune problems including demodex, missing teeth, malocclusion (overbite or underbite), cardiac problems, epilepsy, progressive retinal atrophy (PRA), cataract, and small ear canals with a tendency for infection. As with most large breeds, some will suffer with elbow or hip dysplasia, although this has not been a major problem in the Tibetan Mastiff. Another concern includes canine inherited demyelinative neuropathy (CIDN), a rare inherited neural disease that appeared in one bloodline in the early 1980s.

Canine Hip Dysplasia (CHD) takes many forms, e.g., the femoral head ("ball") may not fit well into the acetabulum ("socket"); the ligament connecting the two may be lax, allowing dislocation; there may be no femoral head at all. Not all forms cause clinical signs. Very active, well-muscled dogs with no femoral heads may show no impairment. Their owners may be unaware of their dogs' "hip dysplasia" unless/until there is a reason to x-ray the hips.

As with all dog breeds, hip dysplasia is caused by the interaction of genes and environment. Inheritance of CHD appears to be polygenic, i.e., it is caused by more than one gene. Mode of inheritance (dominant, recessive, dominant with incomplete penetrance, etc.)has not been determined but may be different in different breeds. Rapid growth and weight gain in puppies may trigger or exacerbate a genetic tendency to all sorts of skeletal problems. Many TM breeders recommend against feeding "puppy food" and especially against feeding "large-breed" puppy food, as these concoctions may contain too many calories, leading to fat puppies. Some breeders and owners believe that supplementation with Vitamin C may prevent the development of CHD even in dogs with the genes for it.

Canine Inherited Demyelinative Neuropathy is an inherited condition that appeared in one of the prominent lines of Tibetan Mastiffs in the early 1980s. CIDN affect the peripheral nervous system. Nerve fibers are unable to transmit impulses from the spinal cord to the muscles because of the breakdown of the myelin sheath. Starting at approximately six weeks of age, affected pups begin to lose the ability to walk or even stand. Progression of the condition can take anywhere from a few days to two weeks. Information from "The Tibetan Mastiff" by Ann Rohrer and Cathy J. Flamholtz

Because this condition is inherited as a simple autosomal recessive, it is virtually impossible to completely eliminate it from the gene pool. One known carrier was bred to over 30 times, producing at least 134 direct descendants. Many descendants of this dog are still being bred so there is always the risk - however slim - of producing more affected puppies. Breeders need to be cautious about pairing up any two descendants of this dog...

Hypothyroidism is fairly common in Tibetan Mastiffs, as it is in many large "Northern" breeds. TMs should be tested periodically throughout their lives using a complete thyroid "panel". (Simple T2/T4 testing is virtually useless...) However, because the standard thyroid levels were established using domestic dog breeds, test results must be considered in the context of what is "normal" for the breed, not what is normal across all breeds. Many TMs will have "low" thyroid values but no clinical symptoms. Vets - and owners - differ on the relative merits of medicating dogs who "test low" but are completely asymptomatic. Some researchers think that asymptomatic hypothyroidism may have been adaptive in the regions of origin for many breeds, since less nutrition is required for the dog to stay in good condition. Therefore, attempts to eliminate "low thyroid" dogs from the TM gene pool may have unintended consequences for the breed.

In affected dogs, symptoms may include decreased activity and playing, increased sleeping, weight gain, poor skin and coat condition such as flaking and scaling, a "yeasty" smell to the coat, frequent ear infections, and negative changes in temperament. Fortunately, this condition is easily treated by the use of daily thyroid supplementation.

Osteochondritis Dessicans is a skeletal defect in which the cartilage lifts off the bone, becomes thickened and cracked, causes inflammation and pain, and in severe cases degeneration of the joint. This conditions strikes males more than females. Keeping an affected puppy lean may help but surgery may be required to relieve pain.

Panosteitis is inflammation of the bones that strikes young dogs. The animal will become lame in one leg and then the inflammation will shift to a different leg. This is one condition that corrects itself over time, and only pain medication is needed.

Hypertrophic Osteodystrophy (HOD) is a condition that affects young large breed dogs. It is very painful and prognosis is fair to poor due to recurring episodes of the condition. Clinical signs of HOD include fever, lack of appetite, and depression. Lameness may vary from mild to severe. With multiple limbs affected, the dog may be reluctant to stand or walk. HOD may be mistaken for Panosteitis without proper diagnosis.

Treatment is only supportive. Intravenous fluids are usually required to keep the patient hydrated. Nutritional support is provided with a feeding tube if the dog refuses to eat for five or more days. Pain is controlled with narcotics and NSAIDs. Antibiotics are used if the dog has signs of pneumonia or other bacterial infections. If the bones become twisted due to growth plate damage, corrective surgery may be indicated. Because the distemper vaccination has been implicated, inoculation should be delayed until the pet has been in remission for a couple of months. Information from http://www.

vetsurgerycentral.com/hod.htm

Ear Infections can be serious and the dog should be taken to the vet if you see it shaking its head or scratching more than normal. Tibetan Mastiffs have pendant ears, making them more prone to ear infections. The vet needs to determine the cause, and may prescribe antibiotics and/or ear drops. Some ear infections are contagious to other dogs if they involve mites or some bacteria.

History

This is an ancient breed. It has been theorized that an early Tibetan dog is the ancestor to all Molossuses breeds. A study at Nanjing Agricultural University's Laboratory of Animal Reproductive Genetics and Molecular Evolution in Nanjing, China, found that while most common dog breeds genetically diverged from the wolf approximately 42,000 years ago, the Tibetan Mastiff genetically diverged from the wolf approximately 58,000 years ago.

Many Tibetan Mastiff breeders and owners (and their web sites) claim that Marco Polo encountered the large Tibetan dogs in his travels and described them as "tall as a donkey with a voice as powerful as that of a lion." However, reading of Polo's works does not support this. In fact, other travels told Marco Polo about these enormous dogs - and about unicorns and other exotic creatures.

In the early 19th century, King George IV owned a pair of TMs, and there were enough of the breed in England in 1906 to be shown at the 1906 Crystal Palace show. However, during the war years, the breed lost favor and focus and nearly died out in England.

After 1980, the breed began to gain in popularity worldwide. Although the breed is still considered somewhat uncommon, as various registries and show organizations (FCI, AKC) began to recognize the breed, more and more active breeders have arisen. Initially the breed suffered because of the limited gene pool from the original stock, but today's reputable breeders work hard at reducing the genetic problems through selective breeding and the international exchange of new bloodlines.

In 2008, the Tibetan Mastiff competed for the first time in the Westminster Kennel Club Dog Show.

In recent years, more wealthy Chinese are buying Tibetan Mastiff as a means to show off their status. It was reported in Sep 2009 that a rich Chinese woman spent more than USD 600,000 or 4 million yuan to buy an 18 month old purebred male Tibetan Mastiff, which she named Yangtze No. 2. This is - purportedly - the most ever paid for a dog.

See also

- Dog
- Index of Tibet-related articles
- Dog of Osu

References

- Alderton, David (1984). *The Dog*.
- Fogle, Bruce, DVM (2000). *The new Encyclopedia of the Dog*. Doring Kindersley (DK). ISBN 0-7894-6130-7.
- Palmer, Joan (1994). *The Illustrated Encyclopedia of Dog Breeds*. ISBN 0-7858-0030-1.
- Schuler, Elizabeth Meriwether (Ed.) (1980). *Simon & Shuster's Guide to Dogs*. ISBN 0-671-25527-4.
- 倪正, (2000). "真实的藏獒(The Real Tibetan Mastiff)". ISBN 7-80173-535-8

Article Sources and Contributors

Breed Groups (dog) *Source*: http://en.wikipedia.org/?oldid=371298317 *Contributors*: 1 anonymous edits

American Kennel Club *Source*: http://en.wikipedia.org/?oldid=373448194 *Contributors*: 07bargem

Working Group (dogs) *Source*: http://en.wikipedia.org/?oldid=362528427 *Contributors*: 1 anonymous edits

American Akita *Source*: http://en.wikipedia.org/?oldid=372510507 *Contributors*: 1 anonymous edits

Alaskan Malamute *Source*: http://en.wikipedia.org/?oldid=374173472 *Contributors*: Howlatthemoonmalamutes

Anatolian Shepherd Dog *Source*: http://en.wikipedia.org/?oldid=374896139 *Contributors*: 1 anonymous edits

Bernese Mountain Dog *Source*: http://en.wikipedia.org/?oldid=376102589 *Contributors*: 7&6=thirteen

Black Russian Terrier *Source*: http://en.wikipedia.org/?oldid=375353116 *Contributors*: Andrmoljak

Boxer (dog) *Source*: http://en.wikipedia.org/?oldid=376410263 *Contributors*: Dirkbb

Bullmastiff *Source*: http://en.wikipedia.org/?oldid=368592614 *Contributors*: SlimVirgin

Doberman Pinscher *Source*: http://en.wikipedia.org/?oldid=376419598 *Contributors*: Peter cohen

Dogue de Bordeaux *Source*: http://en.wikipedia.org/?oldid=373359233 *Contributors*: 1 anonymous edits

German Pinscher *Source*: http://en.wikipedia.org/?oldid=376392608 *Contributors*: 1 anonymous edits

Giant Schnauzer *Source*: http://en.wikipedia.org/?oldid=366006080 *Contributors*: 1 anonymous edits

Great Dane *Source*: http://en.wikipedia.org/?oldid=376289166 *Contributors*: DavidOaks

Great Pyrenees *Source*: http://en.wikipedia.org/?oldid=373674293 *Contributors*: 1 anonymous edits

Greater Swiss Mountain Dog *Source*: http://en.wikipedia.org/?oldid=374314949 *Contributors*:

Komondor *Source*: http://en.wikipedia.org/?oldid=376298555 *Contributors*: 1 anonymous edits

Kuvasz *Source*: http://en.wikipedia.org/?oldid=373296965 *Contributors*: 1 anonymous edits

English Mastiff *Source*: http://en.wikipedia.org/?oldid=374486331 *Contributors*: Collieuk

Neapolitan Mastiff *Source*: http://en.wikipedia.org/?oldid=375195297 *Contributors*: Woohookitty

Newfoundland (dog) *Source*: http://en.wikipedia.org/?oldid=375701379 *Contributors*: 1 anonymous edits

Portuguese Water Dog *Source*: http://en.wikipedia.org/?oldid=375746225 *Contributors*: Angelzoey2

Rottweiler *Source*: http://en.wikipedia.org/?oldid=376339467 *Contributors*:

St. Bernard (dog) *Source*: http://en.wikipedia.org/?oldid=376038442 *Contributors*: The Blade of the Northern Lights

Samoyed (dog) *Source*: http://en.wikipedia.org/?oldid=376682696 *Contributors*: Graham87

Siberian Husky *Source*: http://en.wikipedia.org/?oldid=376688587 *Contributors*: 1 anonymous edits

Standard Schnauzer *Source*: http://en.wikipedia.org/?oldid=365529885 *Contributors*: 1 anonymous edits

Tibetan Mastiff *Source*: http://en.wikipedia.org/?oldid=372808214 *Contributors*: 1 anonymous edits